HIDDEN
HISTORY
of
EAST TEXAS

Tex Midkiff

THE
History
PRESS

Published by The History Press
Charleston, SC
www.historypress.com

Copyright © 2020 by Harold Midkiff
All rights reserved

Cover image: The Francis Henry Midkiff family at their homestead, known as Sandhill, near Bedias, Texas (circa 1900). *Author's collection*.

First published 2020

Manufactured in the United States

ISBN 9781467146036

Library of Congress Control Number: 2020934431

Notice: The information in this book is true and complete to the best of our knowledge. It is offered without guarantee on the part of the author or The History Press. The author and The History Press disclaim all liability in connection with the use of this book.

CONTENTS

CONTENTS

ACKNOWLEDGEMENTS

First, I want to thank my beautiful and supportive wife, LaJuana. After my first marriage, I wrote a book titled *Divorce Made SIMPLE (In 100 Difficult and Very Expensive Lessons)*. In that book, I made the observation that "I'd never let a rattlesnake bite me twice!" I didn't. LaJuana has been the best thing that ever happened to me. She is my best friend, soul mate and, most importantly, the person who won't hesitate to tell me when I'm wrong. Without her, this project would not have been possible. Thank you, my love.

Chuck Roy and Sharon Feldt are my literary heartbeat. Their advice and counsel have been invaluable, as they have pushed me to be a better writer. A kind word of praise from true writing professionals goes a long way. Even editors can have a heart.

My good friends Gary Williams and Bonnie Woolverton have kept me factually accurate and inspired me to conceive this anthology in my curious and humorous writing style. History has a way of looking back "through the rearview mirror," and I trust them to keep the car on the road.

My breakfast companions at the "Table of Knowledge" in the Yantis Café keep my ego in check and make sure that I don't have any trouble getting my "big" head through the door. Likewise, the 1968 graduating class of Palestine High School, led by Don and Millye Bailey, make sure that I stay true to my small-town East Texas roots.

INTRODUCTION

When you live in part of a state that you love more than all the rest, you can't help but want to know: "How did it get so great?"…"Who is responsible?"…"How was I lucky enough to be born here?" I'm talking about East Texas of course!

This anthology starts in deep East Texas with the French explorer La Salle; travels west to Austin, where George Armstrong Custer was stationed; meanders over to Bryan, the last meeting place of Hood's Texas Brigade; and then follows the Trinity River north to Dallas, where the world changed in 1963.

This history of East Texas introduces you to notable but lesser-known characters: Candace and Peter Ellis Bean, Old Rip, Jack Lummus and Vernon Wayne Howell. Remarkable places of interest on this journey include Buttermilk Creek, the Aurora crash site, the Reo Palm Isle and La Grange, Texas. All in all, this portal to the past is hotter than miss Edna's parlor at the Chicken Ranch and sweeter than the sweet potatoes in Golden and covers more towns than Johnny Cash's classic hit "I've Been Everywhere."

Well, about now, you're maybe wondering where the hell is East Texas? When an East Texan meets someone new (especially a non-Texan) and they ask them where they live, they usually respond Arbala, Yantis, Golden or some other unique community in the area. The next question is, obviously, "Where is that?" Almost immediately, they respond, "East Texas!" But wait a minute, East Texas is more than 385 miles wide (Brady

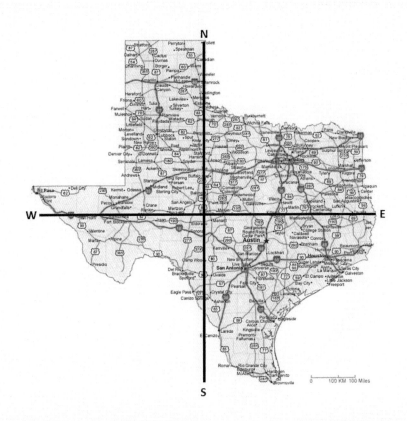

The four quadrants of Texas. *Author's graphic.*

to Burkeville) and 665 miles long (Powderly to Brownsville). That's an area bigger than forty-seven states. Only Alaska, California and Montana are bigger than East Texas!

If you are asking, "How can that be?" simply take a map of Texas and divide it into four quadrants by distance. It will look something like the map above. Now it becomes apparent that East Texas is a pretty big place, and yet, just half the size of the great state of Texas.

There are more than 70,000 miles of highway in Texas, of which 40,985 are paved farm and ranch roads. Besides Texas roads, there are more than 1 million signs and markers. Texas uses 1.6 million gallons of white and yellow paint each year to paint stripes along its highways. After the popularity of the song "Luckenbach, Texas," so many road signs were stolen that the government stopped making them.

8

According to the Texas Almanac, the Lone Star State extends 801 straight-line miles from north to south and 773 miles from east to west. Austin is closer to New Orleans than it is to El Paso, and San Diego is closer to El Paso than Houston is. Houston to New York City is a 1,628-mile drive, give or take a few detours. That's like driving from Houston to El Paso and back.

You may be more accurate in describing your location to your new friend by limiting your response to just one quadrant, but each quadrant averages 6,700 square miles. For instance, the Southeast Texas Quadrant is home to the famous "King Ranch." The King Ranch is bigger than the entire state of Rhode Island. Known as the "birthplace of Texas ranching," it is 825,000 acres or 1,289.06 square miles. Three of the top eleven largest cities in the nation (Houston, San Antonio and Austin) are in this sector.

The Southwest Texas quadrant includes Brewster County, the largest county in Texas. It measures 6,193 square miles, which is roughly the size of Connecticut. Delaware could fit inside Brewster three times. The Big Bend National Park, also located in this sector, is the second-largest but one of the least visited national parks in the contiguous United States.

About 90 percent of the world's recoverable helium is in the ground under Amarillo in the Northwest quadrant of Texas. Geologists also say that a new survey showing an oil field in this sector dwarfs others found so far, according to the U.S. Geological Survey. The Midland Basin of the Wolfcamp Shale area in the Permian Basin is now estimated to have 20 billion barrels of oil and 1.6 billion barrels of natural gas. This estimate would make the oil field, which encompasses the cities of Lubbock and Midland (118 miles apart), the largest "continuous oil" discovery in the United States.

Now that we have at least determined the greatness and expanse of three of the four quadrants of Texas, we can narrow down the description of where they live to Northeast Texas.

Some folks in the area will say that they live so many miles east of Dallas because of the popularity of the TV show. This series debuted as a five-part miniseries in 1978, but the show's unexpected success subsequently turned it into a regular series for the next thirteen seasons. The show has been broadcast in more than ninety countries and dubbed into sixty-seven languages. Larry Hagman (J.R. Ewing) was the only actor to appear in all 357 episodes. His signature cowboy hat is currently held in the Smithsonian's National Museum of American History's collections.

Since Dallas is more than two hours from most of us in this community (three hours if you are trying to make a flight at DFW), it doesn't seem to be an accurate descriptor for someone who you may now want to call a friend.

Besides, if they have ever picked anyone up at this airport, they will know that the Dallas/Fort Worth International Airport is home to the world's largest parking lot.

My pick for a well-known location that will stimulate their brain to picture where we live in this great state of Texas is Tyler (home of the "Tyler Rose," Earl Campbell). If they aren't pro football fans—and some are not these days—you can tell them it is also the home of the Tyler Municipal Rose Garden (the world's largest rose garden). It contains thirty-eight thousand rose bushes representing five hundred varieties of roses set in a twenty-two-acre garden. I like to say I live about an hour north of Tyler.

Where is East Texas, you are probably still asking? The truth is that it can be anywhere between Quanah, Texarkana, Port Arthur and McAllen, but its "drop dead center" is Franklin, Texas.

When people ask me, "Why do you write about East Texas history?" I fervently reply, "Because somewhere down the line some liberal revisionist is gonna want to change the story to fit his or her political agenda. It ain't gonna happen on my watch!"

PART I

BEFORE 1850

ANCIENT TEXANS

Everybody loves East Texas—even the people who were evading the vast glacial thaws and pushing animals of all kinds south some twenty-one thousand years ago. The earliest people who lived in what we now call Texas showed up during the later stages of the ice age. Scientists can identify them by the kinds of weapons they made for hunting. Archaeologists have found this evidence by looking at several types of sites, including campsites, where people lived; quarries, where people cut away material to use as tools; kill sites, with evidence of hunters and the remains of their prey; and cave painting sites.

Gault Assemblage of Tools, 19,700 BC

As recently as July 2018, a research team led by Thomas Williams from the Department of Anthropology at Texas State University, working at the Gault Site near Florence, northwest of Austin, dated a significant assemblage of stone artifacts to sixteen thousand to twenty thousand years of age, pushing back the timeline of the first human inhabitants of North America. Williams's team of archaeologists excavated the Texas bedrock and uncovered ancient rocks shaped into bifaces—used as hand axes—blades,

Gault archaeological excavation site in East Texas *Wikimedia Commons.*

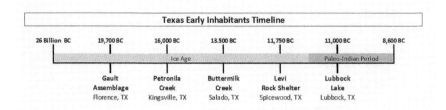

Author's graphic.

projectile points, engraving tools and scrapers. They refer to the tools as the Gault Assemblage.

According to *Science News*, "the team used optically stimulated luminescence to age the materials, which means they were able to find how long it had been since the sediment the items were found in had been exposed to sunlight." Not much about the physical traits of the people who used the tools can be determined from the material in the find, but its significance lies in how old the items are. The team does not claim to have answered the question, "Who were the first Americans?" But the find illustrates the presence of a heretofore unknown "projectile point technology" in North America long before any previously dated sites.

Petronila Creek Mammoth Bones, 16,000 BC

Humans were occupying a hunting and fishing camp on Petronila Creek, between Kingsville and Corpus Christi, eighteen thousand years ago. They were hunting for mammoth, ground sloth, camel, horse, peccary, antelope, coyote, prairie dog and alligator, as well as fishing for catfish, gar and other fish.

A "bone bed" was found at this site that contained some of the largest mammoth femurs (1,429mm/400mm) ever found in North America and included "cut marks" from sharp stone tools. The Petronila Creek site was important at the time because it preceded the advent of the "Clovis" culture by seven thousand years.

Buttermilk Creek Hunter-Gatherers, 13,500 BC

On March 25, 2011, along with colleagues, archaeologist Michael R. Waters, director of the Center for the Study of the First Americans at Texas A&M

University, reported that excavations at the Buttermilk Creek Complex at the Debra L. Friedkin Paleo-Indian archaeological site in present-day Salado showed that hunter-gatherers were living at this site and making projectile points, blades, choppers and other tools from local chert for a long time, possibly as early as 15,500 years ago.

More than fifteen thousand artifacts were embedded in thick clay sediments immediately beneath typical "Clovis" material. These discoveries predated the arrival of the Clovis people from Asia and confirm the emerging view that people occupied the Americas long before what scientists had previously determined.

Levi Rock Shelter, 11,750 BC

The Levi Rock Shelter, named for former property owner Malcolm Levi, is an archaeological site near Spicewood in western Travis County. Located along Lick Creek, the site was excavated on three occasions (1959–60, 1974 and 1977) under the direction of Herbert L. Alexander Jr. He collected considerable evidence of the use of this shelter in pre-Paleo-Indian times. A travertine deposit containing bone and flakes against the back wall is apparently the oldest deposit in the shelter.

A sparse lithic assemblage and bones of deer, rabbit, bison, dire wolf, horse and other species were recovered. This site also contained bones of extinct animals, including bison, peccary and tapir. Alexander is credited with discovering the "Levi Point" (also known as Plainview-Angostura arrowheads). Two types were found at this site. One was a lanceolate form, and the other was a constricted stem point. Both points were thought to be made by the same localized group.

Lubbock Lake Bison Bones, 11,000 BC

Apparently, an ancient tribe with no sense of direction missed East Texas and wandered over to the next watering hole! In 1936, the City of Lubbock dredged the meander of the Yellow House Draw, also known as "Punta de Agua," a tributary of the Brazos River, to make it a usable water supply. These efforts were unsuccessful but brought to light the archaeological significance of the site. The first explorations of the site were conducted in 1939 by the West Texas Museum, now the Museum of Texas Tech University. In the late 1940s, several bison kills were discovered. These charred bison bones produced the first-ever radiocarbon date.

Like at all these archaeological sites in Texas, the smallest artifact can be a crucial clue to unraveling a "day in the life" of an ancient Texan—a bison kill, an overnight camp, a projectile point providing a meal—sealed by the almost unbroken deposition of windborne dust, overbank flood mud or pond and marsh deposits.

It is comforting to think that the oldest inhabitants of North America chose East Texas to make their homes. Contrary to popular belief, the oldest Texans are not those guys surrounding the "Table of Knowledge" at the Yantis Café each morning.

A French Whodunit and a Texas Wherewasit

Mystery of the Explorer La Salle's Last Resting Place

In the tenth or eleventh grade, while studying European exploration of the New World, you probably came across the French explorer René-Robert Cavelier, Sieur de La Salle. If your memory is somewhat available from that period when you passed notes in study hall and stuck chewing gum to the bottom of your desk, then you might recall that he was on an expedition in Texas when someone killed him and disposed of his body. To this day, history has fallen a little short on the "whodunit" or the "wherewasit." The fact that La Salle's death occurred in 1687, before satellite imaging and GPS positioning, not to mention the television show *Expedition Unknown*, contributes to the mystery.

What we do know is that on July 24, 1684, La Salle set out for North America with a large contingent of four ships and three hundred sailors to establish a French colony on the Gulf of Mexico at the mouth of the Mississippi River and challenge Spanish rule in Mexico.

The expedition was doomed from the very beginning. La Salle argued with the marine commander over navigation. Pirates took one of his ships in the West Indies. When the fleet landed at Matagorda Bay (near present-day Port O'Connor), they were five hundred miles west of their intended destination. There, a second ship sunk and a third headed back to France. A

Nineteenth-century portrait of René-Robert Cavelier, Sieur de La Salle. *Wikimedia Commons.*

drunken pilot wrecked the last ship, stranding the remaining crew on land. In October of that year, La Salle took a small contingent of men and headed up the Lavaca River, trying to locate the Mississippi. After most of his men were lost, he continued with about thirty men until a mutiny erupted.

On March 19, 1687, he was slain by one of his own men during an ambush. According to a written account of one of the survivors, they were "six leagues" from the westernmost village of the Hasinai (Tejas) Indians. Historians differ on which of his men pulled the trigger on La Salle, but the preponderance of the evidence rests with Pierre Duhaut, aided by Jean L'Archevêque.

This may have been the first known murder of a Caucasian male in East Texas, but the lasting mystery continues to be a Texas "wherewasit." At least eight communities in Texas have made claims as "the place where La Salle was killed."

Alto, Texas

An area near the town of Alto is one of the contenders for this debatable honor. The late F.W. Cole, a Cherokee County historian, did considerable research of La Salle's movements in East Texas. He concluded that La Salle was killed on the east bank of Bowles Creek in the Martin Lacy Survey two and a half miles southeast of Alto.

In an article originally published in the *Rusk Cherokeean* and later printed in *Two Hundred and Fifty Years: History of Alto, Texas, 1686–1936,* Cole contended that La Salle could not have been killed near Navasota but was instead murdered somewhere near the Neches River. His thorough inspection of French records shows that La Salle's expedition crossed the Colorado River on January 27, the Brazos River on February 9, the Trinity River on March 6 and the Neches River on March 14, 1687. Cole placed the murder site as two to three leagues (a league being about three miles) northeast of the point where La Salle crossed the Neches, or just south of what was once Harrison's Branch, in the Martin Lacey Survey in Cherokee County.

Beaumont, Texas Country Club

Another claim to the historic murder site has been made by the Weiss family of Beaumont. What makes this claim unusual is that the family places La Salle's death at the current location of the Beaumont County Club. A few historians have asserted that the murder took place at "a crossing about fifty miles up the Neches river," and the Beaumont Country Club would fit this description.

The arguments for this site revolve around the "excellent camping grounds" and "high banks affording safe landing," plus the fact that the Beaumont Country Club marks an ancient crossing of the Neches long known as Collier's Ferry. As you stroll up the eighteenth fairway, you may be walking in the shadow of what the French courtiers called the "Adventurer."

Burkeville, Texas

In 1913, Jasper native Jesse J. Lee wrote a letter to a friend at the University of Texas claiming that a camp of German stave makers (whiskey barrel parts) cut down a large white oak tree near Burkeville, in Newton County,

Texas, and found carved in its trunk the words "La Salle." This led to local speculation that La Salle may have been killed near the Sabine River. This historic crossing, which is now called Burr's Ferry Bridge, is where LA 8 meets Texas State Highway 63 at the Louisiana and Texas state line between Burkeville, Texas, and Burr Ferry, Louisiana.

Hainesville, Texas

This community became famous as a possible burial site in 1870, when excavations were being made for the Haines mill. Ditch diggers uncovered some twenty-five old rifles and later the unmarked grave of a white man interred in a hewn-log coffin near the Joe Moody farm. Speculation had it that the body was that of the French explorer La Salle. Another theory advanced in the 1950s suggested that the remains were those of a member of the Moscoso expedition. Because of the lack of conclusive evidence, both legends have been generally discounted. Further research suggests that the rifles dated from the 1700s and not the 1500s, as previously believed.

Navasota, Texas

One of the most convincing claims to the French explorer's killing field is from Navasota. So certain of their historical assertion, the Texas Society of the Daughters of the American Revolution and the townsfolk of Navasota erected a local statue to the memory of La Salle in 1930. Their claim is strongly supported by a book, *The La Salle Expedition to Texas: The Journal of Henry Joutel, 1684–1687*, edited by William C. Foster. Included in the book is a map indicating that La Salle was ambushed somewhere in western Grimes County, about twelve miles west of Navasota. The expedition crossed the Brazos River on March 14, 1687, and he was killed five days later north of the crossing, according to this account.

Pine Island Cemetery in Vidor, Texas

This is the only cemetery that claims to be the burial site of the famous adventurer. The cemetery isn't located on an island. It was so named because its boundaries fell within a stand of pine trees that grew in the middle of an open prairie, like an island. Just off Mansfield Ferry Road in Vidor, about three-quarters of a mile south of FM 105, the overgrown cemetery is a visual aid to the legend of the French whodunit.

In an interview for an Orange County Historical Society publication in 1976, Marion Stephenson of Vidor said that his grandmother Martha Day Stephenson, who was an Alabama Indian, told him that La Salle and six of his men were buried at the Pine Island Cemetery. Apparently, this was based on stories handed down in her family from generation to generation.

Credibility of the Stephenson family story is supported by an 1897 book by M.E.M. Davis, *The Story of Texas Under Six Flags*. According to Davis, one of La Salle's men, Moragnet (his nephew), had been on bad terms with two others, Jean L'Archevêque and Pierre Duhaut, when they camped "near the crossing of the Neches River." These two murdered Moragnet and an Indian hunter named Nika while they slept. When La Salle went looking for his nephew, they fatally shot him in the head. Davis wrote about La Salle, "He was buried in the lonely spot where he fell.… And so, within the borders of Texas—though the exact spot is unknown— repose the mortal remains of its discoverer."

Rusk County, Texas

Not to be outdone, Rusk has a version of the demise of La Salle. Charlie Langford, a former Rusk County judge, said that his research of Spanish records pointed to an area in East Texas that closely matched Rusk County.

Hardin County, Texas

Kountze, Texas attorney Stanley Coe studied many of the available La Salle documents and concluded that the explorer was killed and buried beside Village Creek in Hardin County. To avoid man-eating Indians on the Gulf Coast, Coe stated that La Salle led his party across what are today's Brazos and Trinity Rivers and reached Village Creek, knowing that it would empty into a river. Coe believed that somewhere on this creek, La Salle was murdered.

Without considering "grassy knoll" conspiracies, we're left with only a few suspects for the French whodunit. Pierre Duhaut, one of La Salle's own crew, allegedly confessed to the assassination. Are we to believe what one Frenchman said about another Frenchman more than three hundred years ago? I think not.

As to the Texas wherewasit, it really doesn't matter, just as long as it's within the borders of this great state. Everything is "bigger" and "better" in Texas, even our stories of exploration, betrayal, murder and French legends. Give a Texan a few random facts and he will come up with a belly-whopper of a yarn that commonly ends with "…and that's the truth, so help me Sam Houston!"

ROCKING THE CRADLE OF TEXAS LIBERTY

In 1936, a Texas Centennial marker was dedicated at the Selman-Roark Cemetery near the old Linwood Community just five miles east of Alto, Texas, on Highway 21. This grave site marker, resting among ancestral oaks, reads in part:

*ONE OF THOSE PIONEER WOMEN WHO BRAVED THE MENACE OF INDIANS
AND FRONTIER LIFE AND ROCKED THE CRADLE OF TEXAS LIBERTY*

Legend has long held that according to her own wish, Candace Midkiff Bean was buried between two trees that she had planted near the Old San Antonio Road. When the straightening of the highway made it necessary to cut down the trees, the actual burial site was lost. In any event, Candace's frontier spirit has been preserved for tourists to visit this site, the oldest cemetery by deed in Cherokee County and one of the oldest Anglo cemeteries in all of Texas.

It was Candace's marriage to the legendary Ellis P. Bean, however, that would take this girl on a historic journey, placing her footprints on the

Texas Centennial grave marker of Candace Midkiff Bean. *Retrieved from findagrave.com.*

Peter Ellis Bean throws a five. *From* Joe B. Frantz's Texas History Movies *(1985)*.

birth of the Lone Star State. When but seventeen years of age, the young Bean traveled from Tennessee to Natchez, Mississippi, where he made the acquaintance of Philip Nolan, then collecting a company of men for the purpose of catching mustang horses in Spanish Territory (Texas). Bean—also known as Peter Ellis, Peter Elias or Pedro—joined the expedition and was elected second in command. On March 21, 1801, near the present town of Tehuacana, Texas, a party of Spaniards overtook the expedition, and Nolan was killed. Bean took charge of the fight, but he and his companions were captured.

Imprisonment lasted until 1811, when the Mexican Revolution offered Bean the opportunity to be released by enlisting in the Royal Army. However, at his first chance, Bean defected to the Revolutionists under General Morelos. The two became fast friends, and Bean displayed such coolness in action that he was promoted to the rank of colonel.

General Morelos directed Bean back to the United States in 1814 to appeal for aid. After a lengthy and dangerous journey, he ended up in New Orleans just in time to join the pirate Jean Lafitte and fight in the Battle of New Orleans (War of 1812) under the command of Andrew Jackson. After the British were defeated, General Jackson granted Bean's request to return to Mexico. News that General Morelos had been taken by the Royalists and shot put Bean on the run again.

Bean himself wrote a comprehensive account of this adventure in 1816 and published it in H. Yoakum's *History of Texas* in 1855 as the "Memoir of Colonel Ellis P. Bean":

I took with me a young lady of fine family, who had lost all they had in the revolution. I married her at a small town on my way, intending to ship her with me to the United States.

This young lady was the lovely Doña Magdalena Falfan de los Godos, a niece of Morelos. She would remain faithful to Bean for the next thirty years, even though most of his time was spent in his new home, Texas.

Bean's escape from the Royalists led him back across the river, finally reaching the residence of his half-brother in White County, Tennessee, in the spring of 1818. According to the *Memoirs of Captain William Shaw, MS*:

> *One of the most respectable and prosperous farmers of White County was Isaac P. Midkiff. His daughter Candace, a diminutive and spirited girl of eighteen became fascinated by the newcomer, Bean, who told strange stories of a far-away land. As the months slipped by in Tennessee, Mexico no doubt seemed farther and farther away to Bean. It is impossible to say whether or not Candace knew of Bean's Mexican wife. If she did, it did not matter, for on an unrecorded date in 1818 there was a wedding and an "infare."*
>
> *After remaining here some time, he formed a matrimonial alliance with a daughter of Isaac Midkiff. He then immigrated with his family and father-in-law to Smackover creek, in Arkansas. Here they settled, without a neighbor within thirty miles of them, and commenced raising stock. At the end of three years, his father-in-law died. This event, together with the news of the liberation of Mexico, and the call for colonists, induced Bean to come to Texas. He located himself at Mound prairie, the ancient town of Texas, and obtained from the Mexican government, for his services, a grant for a league of land including his residence.*

In January 1823, twenty-two years after his first journey with Nolan, Bean and Candace crossed the Sabine into Tejas. It wasn't long (June 1825) before Bean began making regular trips to the south side of the Rio Grande. Arriving back at Mound Prairie from San Felipe after an absence of nineteen months, Bean was furious to find that Candace was demonstrating that two could play the double game, or so he thought.

Excerpts from a letter written by William P. Zuber in 1902 best explain this situation. In detailing the life of Martin Parmer, a signer of the Texas Declaration of Independence and an extraordinary character who was known throughout the West as "the Ring-tailed Panther," Zuber recollected:

> *Now for Bean; he was a bigamist; the Midkiff woman being the junior of two living wives; though it is understood that she was ignorant of the fact when she married him. He bore a commission from the Mexican Federal Government as Indian agent to the Cherokees and other tribes in Texas. This was a military commission and he ranked as a colonel in the Mexican army. This commission was the cause of his residence in Texas, but when in the interior of Mexico, where he spent much time, he claimed a place in that region as his home. At that home lived his senior wife, but I understood that he had no children by her….He made frequent official visits to the city of Mexico, and spent much time with his senior wife. When Texians questioned him concerning his Mexican wife, he replied that he had a woman in Mexico, but not a wife, only a mistress; but men who had been with him in Mexico where his senior wife lived, said that when interrogated there concerning his Texas wife, he answered that he had a woman in Texas, not a wife, only a mistress. Thus he acknowledged both women each in her locality as his lawful and only wife, and doubtless each believed herself to be such.*
>
> *This was the (winter) of 1826. Bean had gone on one of his periodical trips to Mexico. Though the duration of his absence on these trips was always uncertain, it had in this instance been protracted beyond precedent; and some man from Mexico had brought word that he was dead. This news seemed to be reliable, and was fully credited by both his family and the people in general.*
>
> *I now approach the heart of the event. Col. Parmer went to Mrs. Bean's residence, married her and stayed there with her during that day and the night following, also during the second day and night. But on the third day a reliable man came from the west and called to inform him that Bean was not dead. That notable man was alive, in good health and on his way to his Texas home. He had halted at San Felipe where business had detained him during a few days, and the informant had seen him there and talked with him.*
>
> *This intelligence abruptly ended a newly begun wedded life, about forty-eight hours after its commencement. Col. Parmer, probably unwilling for Bean to find him there, departed for his own residence and never returned. One or more days later Bean arrived at home; with what emotions he and his wife met, probably no one but themselves ever knew.*

In 1846, long believing that his father was dead, Isaac Thomas Bean (a son) was convinced by a visitor from Mexico that the missing Bean might still be alive. The stranger's reference to a gold-tipped walking cane and a saddle and silver-mounted bridle (gifts from Jim Bowie) sounded like the colonel's. Isaac immediately set out for Jalapa, Mexico, only to miss his father by three weeks. Death had ended Peter Ellis Bean's turbulent life at the Hacienda La Banderilla in the arms of his Mexican wife. Candace died two years later in 1848.

Bean was no doubt quite a character, but the birth of Texas would not have been the same without these frontier women. In addition to Candace's centennial marker, State of Texas historical markers are located on the site of the Beans' home (1829) four miles east of Nacogdoches and on the site of Fort Teran (which Bean built in 1831), located in what is now Tyler County, about three miles west of Rockland on the Neches Riverbank.

Tejas Explorers or Bad Spellers

How Waco Got Its Name

Whether you pronounce it "wā kō" or "wak ō," the origin of the name of this Central Texas city on the Brazos River is steeped in historical exploration, Spanish translation, Native American migration and cultural literacy.

When Stephen F. Austin's father died and he was left to lead three hundred families into the new Mexican territory in 1822, he looked for men with "pioneer" spirit and not necessarily "men of letters." The land he selected for his colony was along the rich bottomlands of the Brazos, Colorado and San Bernard Rivers. This vast expanse was inhabited by native Indians, among them a Caddoan tribe of the Wichita group known as the Huaco or Hueco (Spanish for "empty" or "hollow"). The main village of this tribe was located near the confluence of the Brazos and Bosque Rivers. It would take a special breed of adventurers to explore and survey this untamed wilderness.

Each farming family received one labor (about 177 acres) and each grazing family one *sitio* (about 4,428 acres). As an additional incentive, each *sitio* was to have a frontage on the river equal to about one-fourth of its length. It's no

Colonel Ellis P. Bean was a U.S. filibuster in Texas and Mexico, as well as a Mexican revolutionary. *Wikimedia Commons.*

surprise that a sizable number of cattle ranches sprang up along the Brazos, even though its owners might previously have been planters in Louisiana, Arkansas or Tennessee. These grantees often wrote to Austin describing their findings in this new world.

One such colonist, Thomas Marshall Duke of Kentucky, made such a report to Austin in 1824 after discovering the Huaco village site (now present-day downtown Waco):

> *This town is situated on the West Bank of the River. They have a spring almost as cold as ice itself. All we want is some Brandy and Sugar to have Ice Toddy. They have about 400 acres planted in corn, beans, pumpkins, and melons and that tended in good order. I think they cannot raise more than One Hundred Warriors.*

The aboriginal origin of the Huaco is unclear. They have been linked to several different tribes, groups and bands roaming the Southwest. As early as 1719, the French explorer Jean-Baptiste Bénard de la Harpe wrote about a settlement of nine tribes that he collectively called "Tonacara." Tribal names of Indians known to live on the Brazos River during this period included Honecha, Houecha, Tawakoni, Tehancanas, Tawehash, Ascanis, Toayas, Qusitas and Yscani—all of which have been linked to the Huaco. It is easy to see how confusing these names were to early explorers.

By 1827, Colonel Ellis P. Bean, filibuster, Mexican revolutionary and Indian agent, was also corresponding with Austin, describing his travels and negotiations in this region of Indian Nations. On June 3, he wrote:

> DEAR SIR *I am happy to inform you that yesterday I have maid Pease with the Waco Nesion and tawacanys also the chiefs of Both nasions is now in this Plase you can treat them as friends and can let your uper setelment now it tomorrow I shall start with them to meet the Comanches and gow with them to Sn. Antonio to settle. All in this thare is nothing worth your notis to Right you all is quiot.*

Austin was resigned to translating Bean's phonetic English, as they had been corresponding for more than a year. It is understandable that he would begin using the spelling "Waco" in his correspondence or on maps when referring to the Indians, the village or the area.

The Huaco eventually moved north, settling near what is present-day Fort Worth, but by 1872, they had ended up in Oklahoma on a reservation with other Wichita tribes. In 1902, they received allotments of land and became U.S. citizens.

Fort Fisher, an outpost for rangers, was the first white settlement established in this area in 1837 but was abandoned after several months. Torrey's Trading Post No. 2 was established in 1844 by George Barnard about eight miles south of the abandoned Indian site on a tributary of Tehuacana Creek. Neal McLennan (for which the county would be eventually named) settled nearby on the South Bosque River. In 1848, a two-league grant of land that included the original Huaco village was sold to John S. Sydnor of Galveston. He partnered with the land agent Jacob de Cordova, Nathaniel A. Ware and Jonas Butler to divide the property and dispose of it at one dollar per acre.

It wasn't until March 1, 1849, that George B. Erath had laid out the first block of a new town at the site. Erath had been one of the rangers who built the fort in 1837, and as a surveyor, he lobbied the new property owners to pick the location of the Indian village as the townsite. Erath, a man not easily dissuaded, also convinced them to change the name to Waco Village from their original choice of Lamartine. When McLennan County was formed in 1850, Waco Village was named as the county seat. Finally, in 1856, Waco Village was incorporated as the town of Waco.

Did Colonel Bean's poor spelling prevent the Baylor Bears from playing their home football games at Floyd Casey Stadium in Huaco, Texas? Maybe.

Boundaries of the Republic of Texas

The shape of the great state of Texas is known around the world. You can ask students in most of the countries on this planet to identify this silhouette, and they will attempt to say "Texas" in English. But did you know that the Republic of Texas included land in present-day New Mexico, Oklahoma, Kansas, Colorado and Wyoming?

That's right. This fledging new county had lots of lands but little money in the coffers. When the smoke cleared at San Jacinto, the defeated Mexican president, General Antonio Lopez de Santa Anna, signed the Treaties of Velasco on May 14, 1836. With this, Santa Anna pledged to withdraw his troops south of the Rio Grande. Setting the Rio Grande as the southern border would begin the boundary from the Continental Divide West, ten miles east of present-day Silverton, Colorado, and follow the course of the river as it flows southward through what is the present-day states of New Mexico and Texas and finally out to the Gulf of Mexico. Its total length was approximately 1,896 miles. This would constitute the southern and western borders.

However, this treaty was never ratified by the Mexican government, and Mexico continued to claim the Nueces River as the boundary. The dispute was not settled until 1848, when the Treaty of Guadalupe Hidalgo was signed, effectively ending the Mexican-American War and firmly establishing the boundary between Mexico and Texas.

The eastern and northern boundary of Texas was set in 1819 by the Adams-Onís Treaty between the United States and Spain. According

International boundary marker with Louisiana. *Wikimedia Commons.*

to this treaty, the border extended from the mouth of the Sabine River north to the 32nd parallel; due north to the Red River; west to the 100th meridian; north to the Arkansas River and present-day Dodge City, Kansas; west to the headwaters of the Arkansas River near present-day Leadville, Colorado; and finally north to the 42nd parallel near present-day Rawlings, Wyoming.

By the end of 1836, the proud new citizens of the Republic of Texas were bragging about a map that looked as follows:

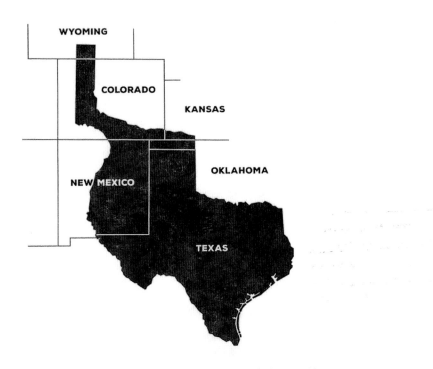

Boundaries of the Republic of Texas from 1835 to 1845. *Author's graphic.*

The familiar shape of today's Texas was defined with the Compromise of 1850, in which Texas gave up its claims to vast tracts of western land in exchange for transferring its crushing public debt to the United States. This debt/land exchange resulted in the modern-day shape of the state of Texas that we all know and love.

This would not be the end of controversy surrounding the borders of Texas. In 1858, when A.H. Jones and H.M. Brown were hired to locate the 100th meridian in making surveys of grants to various Indian tribes, they discovered that the meridian was one hundred miles too far east. The supposedly correct meridian was surveyed in 1860 at the time the Texas legislature decreed Greer County. Because of the Civil War and Reconstruction, Greer County was not organized until 1886. There were two forks of the Red River in this area. The U.S. land commissioner protested the Texas claim. The U.S. Supreme Court settled this dispute in 1896, ruling that the Texas boundary was the south fork (also known as the Prairie Dog Town Fork of the Red River) and the astronomical 100th meridian.

Texas sued Oklahoma in 1920 on the grounds that the surveys of the 100th meridian had erroneously placed that meridian a half mile too far west. Surveys made in 1892 and 1902 did not solve the problem of ownership of an area 134 miles long. One Oklahoma resident complained that she had not moved a foot in forty-five years but had lived in one territory, two states and three counties.

In 1927, the Supreme Court again ordered a survey of the meridian. Samuel S. Gannett worked from 1927 to 1929 to place concrete markers at every two-thirds of a mile. The court ruled in 1930 that the Gannett line was the true meridian. Oklahoma tried unsuccessfully to buy back the strip that the Texas legislature incorporated in 1931 in Lipscomb, Hemphill, Wheeler, Childress and Collingsworth Counties.

My apologies to the good folks of Albuquerque, New Mexico; Hooker, Oklahoma; Dodge City, Kansas; Vail, Colorado; and Rawlins, Wyoming. If Texas hadn't been so broke, you could have all been Texans!

One Old Ranger's Story

The Life and Times of Isaac Jesse Midkiff

Every young boy in Texas daydreams about being a Texas Ranger when he grows up, or at least about being descended from someone like the Lone Ranger. My dream was realized after a research visit to the Texas Rangers Hall of Fame and Museum, located on the banks of the Brazos River in Waco, Texas. Isaac Jesse Midkiff (my great-great-great-grandfather) was right there

Texas Ranger, Don Hunt's sculpture of a nineteenth-century ranger on horseback at the entrance to the Texas Ranger Hall of Fame and Museum in Waco. *Wikimedia Commons.*

in the records with the likes of John Coffee "Jack" Hayes, George Erath and "Lone Wolf" Gonzaullas!

Isaac Jesse was born in Sparta, White County, Tennessee, on April 3, 1810. The earliest record of him living in that area is from an 1807 deed that indicated that his father, Isaac P. Midkiff, owned land to the south and west of Daniel Haston's 150 acres in the Big Spring branch area of Cane Creek at the time Daniel purchased his land. Isaac was one of the most respectable and prosperous farmers of the area.

The War of 1812 was a defining period in the early history of Tennessee and for the Midkiff family. As a result of General William Carroll's call in November 1814 for volunteers to defend New Orleans against an expected attack by the British, Colonel James Roulston formed the Third Regiment of Tennessee Militia. Isaac P. Midkiff was in Captain John Townsend's company of this regiment.

On November 21, the regiment left Nashville by boat and arrived in Clarksville on the twenty-fourth. After the British landed about eight miles below New Orleans, General Jackson on December 23 ordered General Carroll and his Tennesseans into New Orleans, to be ready to move at a moment's notice. The British thought that the area next to the swamp was the weakest, but Carroll's Tennesseans were able to stop the attack. There they lived until the battle on January 8. A British officer recorded the skirmish:

> *The whole line from Carroll's Tennesseans to the swamp was almost one solid blaze. Four men deep, the ranks of the Tennesseans never stopped for breath. As fast as one man fired he stepped back for the next to take his place. By the time the fourth line had discharged its rifles, the first was taking aim again. There were barely fifteen hundred rifles in the line yet scarcely a rifle failed to find its mark. The redcoats fell like blades of grass beneath the scythe.*

Isaac P. returned to White County after being discharged from the regiment. In 1818, Isaac Jesse's sister, Candace, a diminutive and spirited girl of eighteen, became fascinated by a newcomer to the area, Ellis P. Bean, visiting his half-brother, Captain William Shaw. Bean, who told strange stories of a faraway land (New Spain), soon married Candace and convinced the patriarch to move the family west.

The family and son-in-law immigrated to Smackover Creek, in Arkansas Territory. Here they settled, without a neighbor within thirty miles of them, and commenced raising stock. They were only about sixty miles from his sister, Heister Midkiff Bunch. At the end of three years, Isaac P. Midkiff died and was buried in an unmarked grave.

This event, together with the news of the liberation of Mexico (1821) and the call for colonists, induced Bean to come to Texas. He located his family (including his wife's mother and siblings) to Mound Prairie, the ancient town of Texas. For his services as Indian agent, he obtained from the government of Mexico a grant for a league of land, including his residence near the current town of Alto.

On December 16, 1826, Benjamin Edwards, Parmer and a group of armed men marched into Nacogdoches displaying a white-and-red flag inscribed with "Independence, Liberty, and Justice." They seized and fortified the "Old Stone Fort" and proclaimed the Republic of Fredonia. With seventy men, including thirty-five volunteers from Austin's Colony, Bean marched on Nacogdoches. At the same time, a small force of Indians threatened the rebels from Ayish Bayou. The Fredonians, realizing that the game was up, evacuated the town and fled across the Sabine.

It is not known whether Isaac Jessie rode with Bean to quell the Fredonian Rebellion, but he was sixteen by that time and many boys that age were stepping early into manhood.

After the Revolution, "Texians" (as they were called) were more reliant on the Texian Rangers than ever before. The "ranging men," organized by Moses Morrison and Stephen F. Austin in 1823, served as needed through the War of Independence. However, the end of the war brought an empty Texas treasury, and the Texian Army was disbanded by 1838. Texas Rangers were often the only force protecting the new republic.

Ranger companies were called by various names: mounted volunteers, mounted gunmen, mounted riflemen, spies and minutemen. Although the names varied, these militia units were similar and performed the same function. These militiamen furnished their own equipment and subsistence. Their mission was to range the frontier, protecting settlers from Indian raids and lawlessness. Periods of service varied from a few days to several months; the pay was poor and often consisted of promissory notes and next-to-worthless Republic of Texas paper money.

Isaac Jessie served several stints in the Texas Rangers, probably due to Indian scares. In 1836, he served in Captain Costley's Company of Mounted Rangers ("to be paid as cavalry") for three months. Costley had recruited a company of men called the First Company of Texas Rangers and served as its captain until December 11, 1836, when Sam Houston discharged him and his company for refusing to obey orders.

Before this less-than-distinguished end to Costley's Rangers, they built a fort (called Fort Houston) in the town square of Houston (in what is now Anderson County, near Palestine). This abandoned settlement should not be confused with the present-day city of Houston, Harris County, Texas. Two walls or stockades, ten feet apart, were built around the fort. Survivors from the massacre at Fort Parker (among them Cynthia Ann Parker's parents) fled to this larger and better fort.

From August 4 to August 21, 1838, Isaac again served his new country, as indicated in the muster roll of Captain H.B. Stephens's Company of Mounted Rangers, Second Regiment, Third Brigade, under the command of Major General T.J. Rusk.

However, having the qualities of a Texas Ranger didn't prevent Isaac Jesse from being accused of being on the wrong side of the law. He apparently got crossways with a Richard Parmalee, a deputy clerk of the court in Nacogdoches County, Texas. "Larceny" and "hog theft" were two court cases filed against him by Parmalee and one of Parmalee's in-laws named Hotchkiss. Isaac Jesse was acquitted on both charges.

It turns out that Richard Parmalee was, in fact, Richard Robinson, a suspected serial killer from New York. In April 1836, Robinson had been surprisingly acquitted of the murder of Helen Jewett, a well-known prostitute in the Fifth Ward brothel district of New York. The murder and subsequent trial filled the New York, Connecticut and Massachusetts papers. The *Albany Evening Journal* called the verdict "a mockery of justice."

After the trial, Richard Robinson, nicknamed now "the Great Unhung," left New York for his parents' home in Connecticut. When an interviewer remarked that the public viewed Robinson as "worse than a savage," he answered, "The public is a damned, long-eared ass." Asked if he thought Helen had loved him, he said, "How could she help it?" About his lie as to the ownership of the cloth cloak, he said, "Deny! Why should I deny—or confess? It was not any of [the police officer] Brink's business to inquire into the state of my wardrobe. I told him a lie because it was natural." Later in the interview, he noted, "They can't prove that I ever saw Helen." Asked if he'd loved her, he said, "Sort of."

The Alamo had fallen in March. Robinson outfitted himself as a soldier and left for Texas in July. On the steamboat *Tuscarora*, Robinson mingled with passengers, joining freely in conversations about the Helen Jewett murder, flirting with young women and talking of his bright future in Texas.

Rejected by the army to fight in the war with Mexico, Robinson settled in Nacogdoches in East Texas, taking the name of Richard Parmalee, using his mother's maiden name. He owned a saloon and billiard hall there and served in 1838 as deputy clerk of the court. Many local people apparently knew of his true identity, and he is reported to have kept a crime pamphlet of the Jewett murder on his parlor table.

After taking ill aboard a steamboat on the Ohio River, he died in a Louisville hotel room of an inflammation of the brain and stomach. An elderly black woman who attended his deathbed said that he was delirious and often ranted about his wife, or so the woman thought, whose name was Helen Jewett. Shipped back to Nacogdoches, his body was given a Masonic burial there.

Helen Jewett was not so honored when she was buried at St. John's Burying Ground on Leroy Street in Greenwich Village. Medical students, notorious grave robbers in her day, dug her up a few nights later—they dissected her body and boiled her bones. The *Herald* reported that they hung her "elegant and classic skeleton" in a closet at the College of Physicians and Surgeons on Chapel Strect, a block from the Park Theater, in Helen's old hunting ground.

The Bedias Road or Bedias Trail, an Indian trail of the time of Spanish and French exploration, connected the Bidai Indian village on Bedias or

Santo Tomás Creek with another settlement at or near the site of present Nacogdoches. The trail crossed the Trinity River at Paso Tomás, the site of Bucareli; passed the Bidai village at the Don Joaquín crossing of the Angelina River, ten miles south of Nacogdoches; and then turned north toward Nacogdoches. This is one of the roads called El Camino Real by the Spaniards, but it was not the same as the Old San Antonio Road, the principal Camino Real of Texas.

Either Isaac Jesse preferred the southern portions of the Bedias Road or he was escaping the troubles Robinson had brought on him; in any case, along with his brother, Henry, and his mother, Susanna, he resettled in Grimes County.

By this time, the area could no longer be classed as a settlement, since most of the families lived north of the present town of Bedias on Sims, North Bedias and Bowman Creeks. The Simes, Bowman, Plaster and Corner families and the Midkiffs were sufficiently close to one another to be considered neighbors. In 1844, Archelaus Bynum Dodson and his wife, Sarah, settled into the neighborhood.

Sarah Dodson had the historic honor of making the first "Lone Star" flag of Texas. In September 1835, when war with Mexico became inevitable, she came up with the idea of making an appropriate flag for her husband's volunteer company. Silk or bunting not available, she designed the flag of alternate squares of blue, white and red calico, with the blue square adjoining the staff. In the middle of the blue square, she affixed a single white star, the design of which was said to be taken from a button on Provincial Governor Henry Smith's coat. This flag flew over the meeting hall on March 1, 1836, where the first Constitutional Convention declared the independence of Texas from Mexico.

Isaac Jesse also obtained land grants with his sister in Leon County, recorded in 1835, in addition to the one with his mother in Grimes County, recorded in 1838. Candace Midkiff Bean owned one thousand acres (including the present-day site of Centerville, Texas), and Isaac Jesse owned a comparable sized adjoining tract.

At the time of Isaac's death, on July 10, 1851, he and his family, including his mother, lived in the northeast part of Grimes County near the old Wilkerson School (known as the Cotton Community) on what would become known to later family members as "Sandhill."

Lost Mexican Treasure in Upshur County

If you are a fan of TV shows like *The Curse of Oak Island*, *Expedition Unknown* or *Detectorists*, you may have the bug to hunt lost treasure but don't want to fly all the way to Nova Scotia. Luckily, you only need to drive as far as Gilmer, Texas! According to legend, there is Mexican gold and silver buried beneath the mud in Little Cypress Creek in Upshur County.

It should come as no surprise that Texans are full of stories about buried treasures that no one has been able to find. Texas has more buried treasure than any other state, with 229 sites within the state's borders. The total value is estimated at $340 million.

Little Cypress Creek rises a half mile east of Ogburn in eastern Wood County (at 32°52' N, 95°12' W) and runs southeast for sixty miles through eastern Wood, central Upshur and western Harrison Counties to its mouth on Big Cypress Bayou, four miles east of Jefferson on the Marion county line (at 32°45' N, 94°15' W).

No legend is worth its salt without a connection to actual historical events, and the "Legend of Mexican Treasure in Little Cypress Creek" is no exception. When Texas became a republic in 1836, after the winning battle at San Jacinto, its independence was never recognized by the Mexican

Cherokee Indian Chief Di'Wali (or Duwali), also known as John Bowles (or Bowl). *Image no. 1/102-661, courtesy of the Texas State Library and Archives Commission.*

government. Not until Texas was annexed by the United States in 1845 and the Mexican-American War of 1846–48 did the Mexicans finally accept defeat. During the nine years between the revolution and annexation, continued threats of a Mexican-Indian alliance kept the settlers in fear across the new republic.

The Mexican government continued to incite the Native Americans to war with the republic. The Mexicans focused their efforts on the Cherokee of East Texas, as they had been migrating to Texas as early as 1807. Promising them both land and money, they soon began to incite some of the renegade factions of the Cherokee to drive the white settlers from the country. These attacks on settlers in East Texas were blamed on a combined Cherokee-Mexican force.

On December 28, 1935, the Provisional Government of Texas appointed Sam Houston, John Forbes and John Cameron as Indian commissioners. It was estimated that there were one thousand warriors, mostly Cherokee, in Northeast Texas, but Henry M. Morfit in his report to Andrew Jackson in the summer of 1836 set the figure at about two thousand.

Houston and Forbes concluded a treaty with the Cherokee on February 23, 1836. The Indians were to be governed by their own laws insofar as those laws did not conflict with the laws of Texas. They were to receive the land they claimed with the provision that any claims before theirs would be respected. The Cherokee and allied tribes would remain within the boundaries designated by the treaty as the San Antonio road and the Angelina, Sabine and Neches Rivers. No other tribes would be allowed to settle in this area, and no individual Indian would be permitted to sell land or white man to buy it.

One week after this treaty was negotiated, the new provisional government of the Republic of Texas named David G. Burnet as its head. Burnet showed no inclination to honor the treaty, and the provisional government did not ratify it. Although Houston was the hero of San Jacinto and was elected president of the republic by a large majority in September 1836, he never won popular or official approval of his Cherokee treaty. He sent the treaty to the Senate on December 20, 1836, with recommendations for its ratification. The Senate took no action on it before Congress adjourned.

Houston's successor, Mirabeau B. Lamar, inaugurated in 1839, quickly announced a policy of favoring total removal of "Sam Houston's pet Indians." After the May 1839 discovery of a letter in the possession of Manuel Flores exposing plans by the Mexican government to enlist the Indians against the Texas settlers, Lamar, supported by popular opinion, was determined to expel the Cherokee.

In July 1839, Kelsey H. Douglass was put in command of about five hundred troops under Edward Burleson, Willis H. Landrum and Thomas J. Rusk and was ordered to remove the Indians to Arkansas Territory. The army camped on Council Creek, six miles south of the principal Cherokee village of Chief D'wila Bowles, and dispatched a commission on July 12 to negotiate for their removal. Chief Bowles refused the terms of the relocation.

The Battle of the Neches occurred a few miles west of Tyler in what is now Henderson County. By sundown, three Texans had been killed and five wounded; the Indians had lost eighteen. The Indians fled, and Douglass made camp. The pursuit was begun on the morning of July 16. A scouting party under James Carter engaged the Cherokee near the headwaters of the Neches River at a site now in Van Zandt County. The Indians sought shelter in a hut and the surrounding cornfields but were forced to abandon them after Carter was reinforced by the arrival of Rusk and Burleson. John H. Reagan, who fought on the Texan side, provided the following account:

Chief Bowles displayed great courage in these battles. In the second engagement he remained on the field on horseback, wearing a military hat, silk vest, and handsome sword and sash which had been presented to him by President Houston. He was a magnificent picture of barbaric manhood and was very conspicuous during the whole battle, being the last to leave the field when the Indians retreated. His horse, however, was now disabled, and he dismounted, after having been wounded himself. As he walked away, he was shot in the back and fell. Then, as he sat up with his face toward us, I started to him with a view to secure his surrender. At the same time my captain, Bob Smith, with a pistol in his hand, ran toward him from farther down the line. We reached him at the same instant, and realizing what was imminent, I called, "Captain, don't shoot him." But he fired, striking Bowles in the head, and killing him instantly.

After the last fighting near Grand Saline, it was estimated that more than one hundred Indians had been killed or wounded in the engagements. As the Cherokee retreated, they were accompanied by the Mexicans, who still carried most of the money that had been promised to the Cherokee in return for driving out the white settlers. Their escape route carried them through present-day Upshur County, where many of them scattered into the swamps and underbrush along what is now known as Little Cypress Creek, north of the present town of Gilmer. The Mexicans, fearing for their lives, were eager to offload the heavy gold and silver coins they carried, as the Texas army was quickly gaining ground. According to legend, the Mexicans hid their cache in a deep spot in Little Cypress Creek.

In no time, word of the hidden treasure spread, bringing dozens of people trying to find the hidden gold and silver. Many still believe today that the Mexican treasure continues to lie beneath the mud of Little Cypress Creek in Upshur County.

The Mysterious Case of the Texas Supreme Court Bible

Sam Houston's Legacy or Legendary Fraud?

In 1845, during annexation into the United States, Austin, Texas, was named the capital of the new state of Texas. The Supreme Court of Texas (SCOTX) is the court of last resort for civil appeals. A different court, the Texas Court of Criminal Appeals, is the court of last resort for criminal matters. An act approved on May 12, 1846, provided that the court should hold its annual sessions at the capital. In November 1850, this was changed by amendment to provide for the court to hold sessions throughout the year in Austin, Galveston and Tyler. This practice continued through secession and the Civil War. The chief justices of the Texas Supreme Court have used a plain, unassuming King James Bible to inaugurate governors and other elected officials since that time.

The court described this Bible as

> *an almost pocket-sized book, bound in simple brown sheepskin—has a plain, hand-drawn cross on the back cover, and an antique Supreme Court seal inked onto on the front. Gently opening the book reveals an inscription on the flyleaf in an archaic hand: "Supreme Court of the Republic of Texas, 184[_]." The last digit is missing— at some point, the page was torn in half, right through the date. Although the Old Testament's imprint was also torn out, the New Testament has its own title page, which states: "Hartford: Printed by Hudson & Co., 1816."*

Portrait of Sam
Houston, taken by
Mathew Brady.
Wikimedia Commons.

An article in the *Austin Daily Statesman* in 1895 stated that this Bible was used to swear in Sam Houston as governor in 1859 and John Hemphill as the first chief justice as early as 1841. In 1955, a *Breckenridge American* story claimed that this Bible had been continuously used in the Texas Supreme Court since annexation.

At the court, the Bible is commonly believed to have once belonged to Sam Houston. Throughout the history of the court, the book has been referred to as the "Sam Houston Bible." George Bush called it "Sam Houston's Bible," and Rick Perry swore on its centuries-old sheepskin four times. But as of late, the court's archivists now say that it's possible that Texas governors have been duped for centuries.

The Argument for Houston's Ownership

Former clerk of the court John Adams led the argument for Houston. He contended that he'd heard about the Houston connection from former chief justice Tom Phillips, who was told by Chief Justice Greenhill that he himself had seen Houston's signature in the Bible on the flyleaf while serving as a briefing attorney in the 1940s. Adams reported:

> *In a meeting with* [former state archivist] *Chris LaPlante, we compared the writing in the Bible and saw that there were some unique characteristics of the writing in the Bible that matched Houston's hand. We agreed that we would not pursue confirmation further than our own opinions but concurred that the writing surely was that of Sam Houston.*

A 1929 *Abilene Reporter-News* article stated that Governor Dan Moody was sworn in with "his left hand upon the Sam Houston Bible." The inauguration information for Governor William P. Clements in 1987 referenced the Bible as belonging to Houston.

Prominent Houston scholar and biographer James L. Haley also agreed that the Bible is an authentic Houston artifact, stating, "I can say with a high degree of confidence that the inscription is indeed in his hand. The formation of the letters is uniformly consonant with all that I have seen, and the rubric, especially, is unquestionably his personal finial."

Mac Woodward, the director of the Sam Houston Memorial Museum, had the chance to see a copy of the flyleaf firsthand and commented, "As far as I could tell, it was Sam Houston's writing….I had the chance to compare it with other copies of his writing and it is identical."

The Argument Against the Bible Belonging to Houston

Twenty-six newspaper articles that span nearly every decade between 1895 and 1975 and discuss this Bible make no mention of Houston's ownership. A 1973 *Austin American-Statesman* feature focused heavily on the Bible, describing the inscription and ripped flyleaf. The articles referred to the "Supreme Court Bible" or the "Bible for the Inauguration"—with no mention of Houston.

Blake Hawthorne, a Texas Supreme Court clerk and the Bible's custodian, put it his way: "You would think that if he [Houston] had given the Bible to the court, and journalists are writing stories about it in the late 1800s, they would have mentioned that."

The missing signature of Houston on the flyleaf has been a bone of contention for decades. According to court archivist Tiffany Shropshire, the torn flyleaf was long blamed on a janitor who, in the 1970s, stole thousands of pages of old Supreme Court archives. But the janitor is off the hook—Shropshire found a 1941 newspaper article that described the torn flyleaf. She also questioned whether Houston even signed the Bible. She noted that letters found in state archives show that the penmanship closely resembles that of John Hemphill, the court's first chief justice.

Verdict

It's anybody's guess—that's why they call it a mystery. The undisputed facts are that it was published in 1816, the binding is original, the book was re-cased and forty-eight governors have placed their left hand on the Bible and taken the oath of office. Despite the mystery, the historic significance of the book is without question. By its very age and provenance, it is an artifact that represents a fascinating period in the history of our state.

In Huntsville, Mac Woodard, the director of the Sam Houston Memorial Museum, summed it up:

> *It's not important to classify it. Whether it was his Bible or the one he used shouldn't be important. The Bible is important because of its connection not only to him but it's connection to the state of Texas and the surrounding community.*

Part II

1850–1900

How the West Was Won: The Telegraph

How the West Was Won is not only a 1962 American Metro color epic western film but also a phrase that represents the question that historians have been trying to answer since the Louisiana Purchase in 1802. Theories abound, including the invention of the "repeating rifle" (Winchester Model 1873), gold and silver rushes, the implosion of the Union that enabled the northern, Republican-controlled Congress to create new western territories, new trails created by cattlemen driving herds to market, the development of "barbed wire" and the expansion of the telegraph.

Popular culture thinks of America's westward expansion as a post–Civil War event, but it had begun much earlier, in the 1850s, when as many as 100,000 migrants flooded into the western reaches of the Kansas and Nebraska territories. "Manifest Destiny" was a phrase that first appeared in print in 1845, in the July-August issue of the *United States Magazine and Democratic Review*. The anonymous author proclaimed "our manifest destiny to overspread the continent allotted by Providence for the free development of our multiplying millions." In other words, it invoked the idea of "divine sanction" for the territorial expansion of the United States. The specific context of the article was the annexation of Texas, which would officially become a state on December 29, 1845.

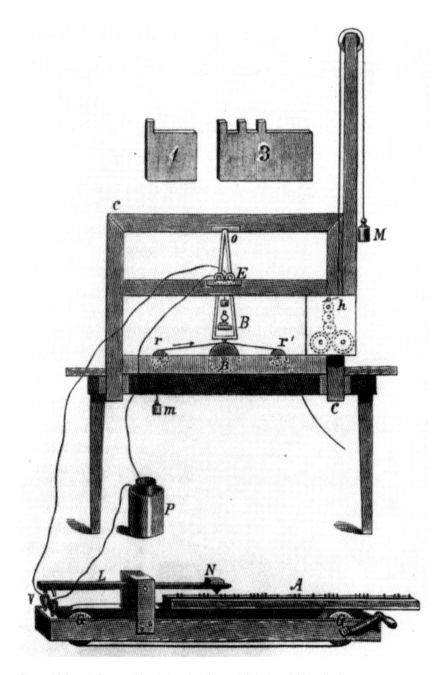

Samuel Morse's first working "electric telegraph" design. *Wikimedia Commons.*

Other applications for Manifest Destiny were soon found. It was used to promote the annexations of Mexican territory acquired in the Mexican-American War, of territory in Oregon gained through negotiations with the British and the seizure (not carried out) of Cuba from the Spanish during the 1850s.

The "electric telegraph," or the telegraph, as it would later be called, was developed by Samuel F.B. Morse and other inventors in the late 1830s. America's first telegram was sent by Morse on January 6, 1838, across two miles of wire at Speedwell Ironworks near Morristown, New Jersey. The message read, "A patient waiter is no loser." Samuel F.B. Morse would be issued a patent, US1647, on June 20, 1840.

One of Morse's first attempts to market his new discovery was to offer it to the Republic of Texas, but the fledging new government failed to recognize its significance. Receiving no reply to his offer, Morris withdrew it in a letter to Sam Houston. This new communication technology would become vital to closing the gap between the East and the West.

The use of the telegraph for communication in Texas, which preceded the railroads and telephone as a national network, began with the chartering of the Texas and Red River Telegraph Company on January 5, 1854. Its first location, in Marshall, was opened on February 14, 1854. Customers were offered connections with New Orleans via Shreveport and with Alexandria, Louisiana, and Natchez, Mississippi. Later that same year, the line was extended to Henderson, Rusk, Crockett, Montgomery, Houston and Galveston. Wires were strung from treetop to treetop. In addition to translating the "Morse code" that came over the line, they would, on many occasions, have to close their offices and ride along the lines to make repairs when the wind swaying the trees led to breaks in the wires.

By this time, Marshall was the fourth-largest city in Texas. Marshall played a major role in the Civil War, providing munitions and manufactured goods for the Confederacy. Marshall became the capital of the Confederacy west of the Mississippi River after the fall of Vicksburg. Marshall continued to thrive thanks in part to it being on a major stagecoach route and a city on the new railroad cutting through East Texas.

The Texas and New Orleans Telegraph Company was chartered on January 15, 1856, and began construction of lines from Galveston to San Antonio and Austin, but it was 1862 before Austin had a direct connection to New Orleans. These first two telegraph companies later consolidated their interests.

There were an estimated 1,500 miles of telegraph wire in Texas by 1874, and Western Union owned 89 of the 105 telegraph offices statewide. Being able to send a message all the way across the country might be expensive, but for distances under 25 miles, telegrams only cost a quarter.

The *Galveston News* was the first Texas newspaper to use the telegraph, using a special leased wire between Galveston and Dallas by 1885. Western Union became the only company operating in the state after its merger with Postal Telegraph and Cable Company, and by early 1949, it employed 2,802 people and operated 1,828 offices in Texas. On February 9, 1972, as part of its decision to close many small local offices around the country, Western Union closed the first telegraph office in Texas at Marshall, which had been in continual operation since 1854.

If you want to learn more about the first telegraph office in Texas, a trip to Marshall is a good bet. Telegraph Park, the site of this historic doorway to one of the legends of "how the west was won," is located downtown on North Washington Avenue. A bronze statue of a telegraph boy takes you back to days long before the cellphone. The Harrison County Historical Museum and the Texas and Pacific Railway Museum is just down the street. In all, Marshall has more than one hundred historical markers and medallions, with several sites listed in the National Register of Historic Places.

BROTHER FOR BROTHER

"E.P. Midkiff reporting for duty, suh," the sixteen-year-old boy, standing at his best attention, barked like an old top rail troop.

"Stand easy boy, there's still some fight left to be had. You'll get your chance soon enough," replied Captain J.W. Hutcheson of Company G, Fourth Texas Volunteer Infantry, from behind his makeshift desk in the command tent.

The citizen-soldiers of this regiment, called the "Grimes County Greys," were primarily recruited in Central Texas under a levy imposed on the state by President Jefferson Davis on June 30, 1861, that called for two thousand troops. Captain Hutcheson's first winter here had been spent in Camps Bragg (nicknamed "Texas") and Dumfries near Richmond, Virginia, where many of his soldiers died from exposure and disease.

Confederate soldiers at Gettysburg. *From Civil War photographs, 1861–65, compiled by Hirst D. Milhollen and Donald H. Mugridge, Washington, D.C., Library of Congress, 1977.*

"Ya got any family here, Private?" asked the lanky captain as he moved his saber to a more comfortable position.

"Yes, suh, my brother…and another man from our parts, Frank Plaster."

"What's your brother's name?"

"Private Isaac Allen Midkiff, but everyone calls him 'Babe.' We lives on Sand Hill near Bedias Crick. Ya know where that is, Cap'n?"

"Yea, I know abouts, I'm from Anderson."

"Yes, suh, that's where I enlisted. A big town in them parts, but nothing like Richmond here."

"Okay. Well, you better get on and find that brother. I know he'll be a want'n to hear news from home." The captain paused but suddenly added, "And don't get'n any trouble!"

E.P., or Pleasant, as his kin back home called him, left the tent and ran right into his brother, Babe. "Well, I'll have to take an image, if it ain't me ugly brother!"

Babe grabbed Pleasant in a bearhug and exclaimed, "I don care what ya call me, I've been wait'n all morn'n to hear about my sweet Mary." Round and round Babe turned Pleasant and wouldn't let go until he finally gave in.

"Miss Wilkerson sends her best. She says she's wait'n for ya, but you'd better hurry up and whip them Yankee boys."

"My sweet darl'n, I can't wait to see her." Babe took off his kepi and held it over his heart. "I hear'd Frank Plaster married our little sister when he got home from Huntsville."

"Yea, but Pa wouldn't let her leave with him until the war's over. Is he here?"

"No." Placing his kepi on the back of his head, in the thinking position, he continued, " I hear he's in the Cavalry, mustered-in at Nacogdoches."

"What outfit is that?"

"Captain M.M. Singletary's Company, Third Regiment, Texas Lancers. I guess he didn't care much for march'n!" Babe took a hard look at his little brother. Taking hold of his arm, he pointed down the camp. "Let's get ya settled in, I see the cracker line just get'n here. We'll see what the latest camp canard is. We might be mov'n out pretty soon."

This camp was like most in the South. Regulations called for the camps to be laid out in a fixed grid pattern, with officers' quarters at the front end of each street and enlisted men's quarters aligned to the rear. It was set up roughly along the lines the unit would draw up in for battle, and each company displayed its colors on the outside of its tents. Mess tents, medical cabins and baggage trains were also located according to the field manual.

Because it was summer, troops slept in Sibley tents, named for its inventor, Henry H. Sibley, who later became a Confederate brigadier general. Made with a large cone of canvas, eighteen feet in diameter, twelve feet tall and supported by a center pole, the tent had a circular opening at the top for ventilation and a cone-shaped stove for heat. As many as twenty soldiers could be assigned to each tent, leading to cramped, uncomfortable quarters. When ventilation flaps were closed on cold or rainy days, the air inside the tent became fetid with the odors of men who had scarce access to clean water in which to bathe.

At the beginning of the war, the Texas Brigade, in which Babe and Pleasant served, was under the command of Brigadier General Louis T. Wigfall. In March 1862, Colonel Hood was promoted to general and given command of the brigade. Babe saw action on the Virginia peninsula on May 7, at Eltham's Landing. Pleasant was sick in Richmond until May 25.

The Grimes County Greys' introduction to real battle came on June 27, at the Battle of Gaines's Mill. Here the Texas Brigade established its reputation for hard fighting by successfully breaking the Union line on Turkey Hill, which had resisted all previous Confederate attempts to do so.

On this day, General Hood dismounted, walked to the front of the Fourth and admonished his men to advance quickly, keep formation and place their rifles at right shoulder shift until they struck the enemy. The sunlight was fading into the west behind the Texans. At Hood's command, Captain Hutcheson and his company dove into the eye of the artillery and small arms storm. Crossing a large field, stepping over the bodies of the dead and wounded, they fixed bayonets and plunged down a ravine into Boatswain's Creek and up the other side. Their eyes were continually searching for soldiers defending the two Union breastworks and cannons on Turkey Hill.

In a letter written the next day by Private Zachariah Landrum of Company H, he explained that Captain Hutcheson was cut down with "grapeshot to the arm and breast" and was removed from the battlefield. Their first captain would later succumb to his wounds.

The now battle-hardened Babe and Pleasant would survive without injury the next three conflicts of 1862: Second Manassas (July), Antietam (September) and Fredericksburg (December). Their new brother-in-law, Frank Plaster, was not so lucky. He was captured at Fort Hindman, Arkansas Post, Arkansas, where his regiment was engaged east of the Mississippi River after a detachment of thirty thousand Union soldiers from the Vicksburg Campaign moved fifty miles upriver to launch a land and naval assault against Fort Hindman. He was a POW imprisoned at Camp Butler, Springfield, Illinois, until he was exchanged in April 1863. Now a sergeant, he was transferred to the Fourth Texas, Grimes County Greys.

On June 26, Longstreet's Corps, including the Fourth, waded the Potomac River at Williamsport on the way to Gettysburg, Pennsylvania. It had poured rain on the troops in Maryland, and now it flooded them in Pennsylvania. They made camp, stacked their rifles, built fires and prepared to cook their rations.

Babe took the ramrod out of his gun, wet up the flour without grease or salt, wrapped it around the black ramrod and held it over the fire. "Ya want some fried bread, brother?"

"No, Babe, I'm a trying to write Sis a letter, and Frank is mess'n with me. He wants me to tell her he's pining away."

"Ya better hurry, I hear'd they're passing out a gill of whiskey to each man. Says General Hood got it, but he ain't tell'n where." Pleasant shrugged and continued writing:

Dear Sister Margaret:

It is once more my privilege to write you a line or two. Since I wrote to you it has been a hard time on the Greys, we have been fighting every few days, Me, Babe and Frank have been through 3 hard battles, not a scratch yet.

Well, Sis, I must say to you we got the letters you, Mamma and Papa wrote, they did us the most good. We have worn them out reading them.

Frank sends his love. He says he started from Texas to find a fight and he has made a success of it. Out here, Frank is like a brother to us.

I am very sorry the family made such poor crops in Tex this season, though I hope you will not suffer for want of something to eat. I must close for this time, I will write often as I can, for the present, fare you well.

Your unworthy brother,

Pleasant

Within a few hours, most of the camp was drunk, including Babe and Frank. One old troop was overheard bragging, "We performed a feat today that is unknown in the history of warfare. We ate breakfast in the State of Virginia, dinner in the State of Maryland, supper in the State of Pennsylvania, and slept in the State of Intoxication!"

By the time the Grimes County Greys reached the foothills near Gettysburg, Hood's Texas Brigade had already fashioned a reputation as perhaps the finest fighting unit in General Robert E. Lee's Army of Northern Virginia. They broke camp and were at Cashtown by 2:00 a.m. on July 2. By 4:00 a.m., they had marched the eight miles to Gettysburg and were cooking breakfast along Willoughby Run, near the John Edward Plank farm.

This farm and every shelter in the surrounding area had been designated temporary hospitals and were filled with bleeding bodies. The surgeons, with sleeves rolled up and bloody to the elbows, were continually amputating limbs. Blood ran in streams from under the operating tables, and huge piles of arms and legs gorily attested to the fierceness of the previous day's battle. It was sure proof that the "ball had been opened."

Babe pulled his wagon into line at Plank's farm. He had been on extra duty as a medical teamster since March 1862. He left to find Pleasant and Frank.

"Y'all had any sleep?" he inquired of the two Rebels sitting next to a smoldering cookfire.

"Nah, but we got some embalmed meat if you want it," Frank replied holding up a tin can.

"I'd about as soon eat my haversack," Babe replied; he paused to listen to the rumble in the distance. Softly, he added, "This is gonna be a tough day, boys. Word is that General Hood is not happy with the way Longstreet wants us to get at them Yankees. John Bell's asked him three times to let us move to the right, but Longstreet says General Lee's orders are to attack on the Emmetsburg Road."

Babe dropped down to one knee and motioned for them to join him. "Let's pray, brothers; I've got to get back to my gut wagon."

By 3:00 p.m., the Confederate line was five to six miles long. The temperature was over ninety degrees. The morning had been spent under what the most experienced soldiers would call the worst shelling they had ever witnessed. When they reached the edge of the timber opposite Little Round Top and Devil's Den, Pleasant could see the Federal batteries, or at least the location of them, by the smoke of discharge. They stood in columns of fours, with their faces toward their right. The Federal battery commenced to play with them—the first shot, which Pleasant recognized, struck the ground about fifty to sixty feet from the line, scattering dust and dirt over the company.

Pleasant saw General Hood on horseback about three or four hundred yards obliquely to his left, just out of direct range of the battery fire, in the edge of the timber. Hood took his hat, held it above him in his right hand, rised to his full height in the stirrups and shouted in a stentorian voice, "Forward…steady…forward!" They all started across the open field. Pleasant heard the words passing down the line, "Quick, but not double-quick!" The sun bared in on Pleasant's face as he began to yell and whoop with the Devil's Den in his sights.

Babe drove his ambulance wagon with a load of wounded up to the Surgeon's tent at Plank's farm. Frank ran up to the wagon seat and cried, "He's dead, he's dead, I found Pleasant near the Devil's Den!"

Babe dropped the reins and moaned the cry of Abraham, "Oh God, oh God, why didn't you…take me?" He was inconsolable, and Frank cupped him in his arms. "What am I gonna tell my Mama. I told her…I told her I'd watch out after my little brother."

After the wagon was unloaded, Babe and Frank returned to the battlefield, collected Pleasant's body and returned to Plank's farm. Babe picked out a reverent spot under an old walnut tree, and they buried him in a shallow grave. Babe said, "We've got to make sure we can find this spot again." He paused, whipping away a tear. "We need to do a real good job in marking it." Frank took out his Arkansas toothpick, found a suitable stone and began to carefully engrave Pleasant's name in large letters.

Prologue

Apparently, Babe and Frank did a "good job" in marking Pleasant's grave site at Plank's farm. Beginning in 1871, Dr. Rufus Weaver was contracted to supervise the removal of more than three thousand Confederate dead left at Gettysburg. Dr. Weaver's men were able to identify Pleasant's remains and moved them to the Hollywood Cemetery in Richmond, Virginia, where he rests along with such notables as Jefferson Davis, J.E.B. Stuart and George Pickett.

Babe and Frank survived the war. Babe was wounded in the leg at the Battle of the Wilderness. They were both in the Grimes County Greys, under General Robert E. Lee, until the Army of Northern Virginia surrendered on April 9, 1865.

After being paroled at Appomattox, Isaac Allen (Babe) Midkiff rode a mule back to Bedias, Texas. As soon as he returned, he married his sweetheart, Mary Wilkinson, on October 25, 1865. They had five children. His first son was named Robert Lee. Babe lived the rest of his life near Bedias, where he was a charter member of the Queen Esther Chapter No. 104, Eastern Star, organized on September 1, 1889. He was "Worthy Patron" in 1892–93. This old Confederate made sure that he attended the annual meetings of the Hood's Texas Brigade Reunion until his death on December 22, 1911.

Henry Franklin Plaster returned to his young wife, Margaret Susanna Midkiff Plaster, Babe and Pleasant's sister. They had fifteen children. He built the first school in the Plasterville Community and opened a store in Bedias. In 1892, he killed Ned Harrison for a remark that, according to the trial transcript, "was a moral attack against the Plaster girls." Frank was acquitted by a jury of his peers and lived in Bedias until his death on January 6, 1905.

Confederate Heroes of Wood County

The bloodiest four years in American history began when Confederate shore batteries under General P.G.T. Beauregard opened fire on Union-held Fort Sumter in South Carolina's Charleston Harbor on April 12, 1861. The next day, U.S. Major Robert Anderson surrendered the fort. Two days later, President Abraham Lincoln issued a proclamation calling for seventy-five thousand volunteer soldiers to quell the Southern "insurrection."

Just one month earlier, Texas governor Edward Clark (who became governor after Sam Houston refused to take an oath of allegiance to the Confederacy) commissioned Samuel Martin Flournoy brigadier general and commander of the Twelfth District, Texas State Troops. Flournoy provided land for Camp Flournoy from his property holdings just southeast of his home in Wood County. This would become the home of Confederate troops in the area and where hundreds of men from Wood County would enlist in the Confederacy.

In August 1861, the new brigadier general wrote to the adjutant general of Texas to report, "In accordance with your instructions, soon after receiving my Commission, I organized my staff by the appointment of J.W. Wilson my aide de

"A Fierce Assault on Port Hudson," newspaper illustration of the attack. *Wikimedia Commons.*

camp; W.J. Sparks Brigadier Major, Howard Keys, Quartermaster F.M. Hays, Commissary, desiring others more essential to the organization of the Militia, Myself, and Staff were immediately qualified in the form of law and our oath of office were forwarded to you in a subsequent communication."

Companies organized by postal service included the First, Captain Wm. D. McKnight (Webster); the Second, Captain D.W. McNabb (Springville); the Third, L.C. Calhoun (Quitman); the Fourth, Captain H.W. Hester (Perryville); the Sixth, Captain T.Y. Logan (Lake Fork); the Seventh, Captain John Benton Sr. (Webster); the Eighth, Captain J.J. Montgomery (Springfield); and the Ninth, Captain W.R. Thorne (Holly Springs). Known as the "Rough and Readies," more than five hundred men from Wood County composed the Twelfth Brigade.

After only seven months as brigadier general, Flournoy enlisted at Camp Flournoy in the Third Texas Confederate Calvary, serving one year as a teamster, using his own team and wagon. After the war, he retired from public service and died at his home in Quitman in 1878. He is buried at the Quitman City Cemetery.

The Tenth Texas Cavalry was organized with about nine hundred men during the late summer of 1861 at Goose Lake (about ten miles northeast of Wills Point) by Colonel M.F. Locke. Many of its members were recruited in the towns of Quitman and Tyler.

Company A (Wood County) was led by Captain Charles D. McKnight. He was listed in the November 30 muster roll as having a $165 horse, a $40 pistol, a $14 sword and a $34 saddle and blanket. First Lieutenant W.S. Trout had a $250 horse, a $60 gun, three $60 pistols, a $10 sword and a $25 saddle and blanket with $5 saddlebags. With all that gear, it is not surprising that he was detailed as a bodyguard for Major Ector in March 1863 and paroled on July 9, 1865, at Marshall, Texas.

Private James L. Ray of Company A was discharged at Meridian, Mississippi, in 1865. He attended the 1903 reunion in Tyler, traveling from Mineola, Texas, and would later become editor of the *Wood County Democrat*. He died in 1929 and is buried at the Texas State Cemetery, Austin, Texas, Confederate Field, Section 1, Row U#11. Another private, J.M. Shipp, was wounded at Chickamauga, Georgia, on September 9, 1863, and was discharged due to the injury. He applied for a pension under the Confederate Veterans Act of 1881 in Wood County and is buried at the Sand Springs Cemetery.

Company B, known as the "Wood County Rebels," was led by Captain John W. Wilson. In a letter to Brigadier General Sibley on August 5, 1861, Wilson closed with, "You please accept us and put us in service just as quickly as possible. We are 'spilling' for a fight." And fight they did. Private A.F. Hamilton was listed as a POW at Citronelle, Alabama, on May 4, 1865. His great-grandson Chuck Carlock would write the book *History of the Tenth Texas Cavalry (Dismounted) Regiment, 1861–1864* in his honor. Wood County Rebel Jacob Ziegler was wounded as a first sergeant on December 31, 1862, but would get back into the war, be promoted to captain and command the Tenth at its surrender at Meridian, Mississippi, on May 9, 1865. He also applied for a pension in Wood County, Texas.

The Second Texas Partisan Rangers was a cavalry regiment that was organized in March 1863 at Fairfield, Texas, under Colonel B. Warren Stone of Dallas. Company A comprised men from Wood County. Stone's Regiment went to Louisiana in May 1863, where it formed in Colonel James P. Major's Cavalry Brigade, a part of General Green's Division. This action put them in direct conflict with General N.P. Banks, the Union commander of the armies that were to invade and occupy Texas. Commodore J.S. Palmer, U.S. Navy, planned to move and supply this army by using about ninety ships traveling up and down the Mississippi River tributaries.

In a letter to his wife on June 13, 1863, Archibald Faulconer, a private in Company A from Wood County, explained that they had been ordered to Port Hudson to "hold at a minute's notice to start." He continued, "If we are cross Bayou Atchafalaya which is a big river 300 yards wide and very deep, we cannot make a retreat safely because there is no bridge to cross it and it is too far to swim." He was basically saying goodbye: "God only knows what may be the result…may go safely and I may not, the chances are against me."

This was some of the most unusual warfare in Civil War history. Stone's Regiment was assigned to harass and attack the Union ships in and around Port Hudson. This regiment of about four hundred of Stone's cavalry rode along the banks of the Atchafalaya, shooting at ships with rifle and cannons. They were continuously engaged in these battles for forty-six straight days, with little food or rest. Literally fighting from their saddles, unit citations for bravery and courage were commonplace. Private Faulconer would survive these initial skirmishes but would be killed in action in 1864.

In the current climate of "political correctness" and "apologetic rhetoric," Wood County can remain steadfast in its remembrance and recognition of these Confederate heroes. They left their homes and farms to fight and die "for the purpose of defending the rights of the States."

Custer's Stand in Texas

Most of us first became aware of General Custer at the movies in such classics as *On the Little Big Horn* (1909), *Custer's Last Stand* (1936) and *They Died with Their Boots On* (1941). Or you might have read about him in your high school American history class, but did you know that he was posted in Texas after the Civil War?

Born George Armstrong Custer in New Rumley, Ohio, on December 5, 1839, the son of Emanuel and Maria (Ward-Kirkpatrick) Custer, he grew up in the area. George realized his youthful ambition in 1857, when he was appointed to the United States Military Academy at West Point. After such an auspicious beginning, he graduated, barely, in 1861 at the bottom of his class.

The Civil War would bring him celebrity as a cavalry officer. At twenty-three, he was made brigadier general of volunteers, and at twenty-five, he earned the rank of brevet major general. George cut a dashing figure with his long blond hair set off by a red tie, a sailor's blouse and a blue jacket adorned with gold. He was nicknamed the "boy general."

Brevet Major General George Armstrong Custer in 1865. *Wikimedia Commons.*

Only a few days after his promotion, he fought at Gettysburg. In this battle, Custer commanded the Michigan Cavalry Brigade and, despite being outnumbered, defeated J.E.B. Stuart's attack at what is now known as the East Calvary Field. Later in the war, his division blocked the Army of Northern Virginia's final retreat, and Custer received the first flag of truce from the Confederates. He was with Robert E. Lee at Appomattox when the South surrendered to Ulysses S. Grant.

In September 1866, Custer, whose regular army rank was captain, was appointed lieutenant colonel of the newly formed Seventh United States Cavalry Regiment. He was assigned to duty in Texas as part of General Philip H. Sheridan's effort to prevent Confederate retrenchment in Mexico under the emperor Maximilian. Lee's surrender ended the Civil War for most people, but Texas was among the states that didn't officially surrender until a month later.

The entire South was ravaged by anarchy in the immediate aftermath of the war. Custer had his hands full maintaining order among his own troops. Custer issued orders that made it clear that "foraging" the land and its bounty would not be tolerated. Anyone found guilty of disobeying those orders would be dealt with harshly.

For his actions, Custer was accused of violating the Reconstruction Laws that "no cruel or unjust punishment" be inflicted on "disturbers of the public peace and criminals." Custer argued that the punishment was neither cruel nor unjust. These orders would protect the Texas planters and farmers from his troops.

Justice was achieved, according to the *New York Times*:

> *Gen'l Custer, knowing that the trial for desertion was a farce, tried every humane way to save his army from going to pieces, but failed. He then tried a new way and flogged several men and shaved their heads. This had the desired effect but brought down the friends of these soldiers upon him, who charge him with being disloyal, inhuman, and everything that is bad. Now, I leave it to everyone if Custer didn't do right.*

On Sunday, August 20, 1866, twelve days after the departure from Alexandria, Louisiana, his cavalry regiment reached Swartwout's Ferry on the Trinity River in Polk County. Officer Browne, one of Custer's staff, kept a journal in which he wrote:

> *We've seen no good country in Texas as yet. Pines and deer, bugs and snakes inhabit the whole face of this place. This country today looks as if it is uninhabited by man, and as if even God himself has abandoned it. There are pines before us, pines behind us, pines on each side of us, nothing but pines.*

The camp was named "Camp Rattlesnake" by the men. Browne's journal continued:

> *One could hardly put their foot down without walking on a snake. We killed one with 14 rattles on his tail and more than six feet in length. Swartwout's Ferry is just a little town, really, too little to mention. We remained in the camp there and dreamed of snakes.*

As they moved south, Browne's impressions of the country began to improve:

> *We made a long march of 27 miles without any water, but on this day we passed through two beautiful villages of Cold Spring and Waverly, the only*

towns that I have seen yet in Texas worth mentioning, after traveling some 150 miles in the state.

Custer's regiment spent two unhappy months in Hempstead waiting for rations that never materialized, so they marched on to Austin. The Custers (George and Libbie) moved into the old Blind Asylum building on the outskirts of town (now restored and a part of the University of Texas campus). The building was a two-story limestone Italianate-style residence that also served as his headquarters. His cavalry camped far less comfortably on the banks of Shoal Creek (roughly parallel to MoPac on the west side of the city now).

Libbie wrote about her experiences in Texas in her book *Tenting on the Plains*. She enjoyed the luxuries of a bathtub, furniture, a fireplace and a social life. As another biographer wrote:

The stay in Austin was an idyllic time, coming as it did between the Civil War and the Indian Wars on the Plains. They spent a lot of time horseback riding and at the race track. Custer liked a little place on Shoal Creek so much that he had a makeshift jail built there. Armstrong was having the time of his life, even while performing the unpleasant and unrewarding task of taming Texas.

Austin was good for the couple while it lasted. George Armstrong Custer was mustered out of the volunteers in February 1867. He would eventually take command of the Seventh Cavalry, meet his fate at Little Big Horn and permanently enshrine his name in the history of East Texas. The Texas legislature passed a "resolution of condolence," noting that Custer had endeared himself to the people of Texas during his brief stay.

BIG TEX AND THE STATE FAIR

If you thought the great State Fair of Texas had always been held in Dallas, you'd be wrong. The original State Fair of Texas was held in Houston from 1870 through 1878. The event, held at historic Fair Park in Dallas, opened its gates for the first time on October 26, 1886, with nearly fourteen thousand people attending.

Big Tex at the State Fair of Texas in 1956. *Wikimedia Commons.*

The twenty-four-day event has taken place every year since except for varying periods during World War I and World War II. It begins the last Friday in September. With an annual attendance of more than 2 million, it is the most highly attended and (some folks say) best state fair in America.

Originally, the fair was charted as a private corporation by local businessmen. It was an immediate success and attracted thousands of people until 1904, when a series of events led to a financial crisis and cost outgrew income. The original investors then sold it to the City of Dallas, with the agreement that twenty-four days during the fall would be set aside annually for the fair and exhibition.

The first quarter of the twentieth century saw new changes to the annual fair. The first designated day for African Americans to attend the fair was held in 1889 and was called "Colored People's Day." Educator Norman Washington Harllee organized exhibits and planned events and speakers, including Booker T. Washington in 1900.

In 1913, the first automobile building was introduced at the fair and was filled with 175 vehicles for fairgoers to see and touch.

The fair was canceled in 1918 due to the U.S. Army taking control of Fair Park to establish an aviation boot camp known as Camp Dick. College football has been traditionally the centerpiece of the fair. As early as 1921, Boston College beat Baylor at the first game ever played between teams from the Southwest and Northeast. Also in that year, Texas and Vanderbilt started a series that was played at the fair every year until 1928 except for 1924. In 1925, the first State Fair Classic was played. The famous "Red River Rivalry" (Texas versus Oklahoma) started in 1929. The stock market crash hadn't taken its toll in the South yet.

In 1930, construction of a new Fair Park Stadium (now known as the Cotton Bowl) began. Texas and Oklahoma continued their Red River Rivalry at the new Fair Park Stadium in 1932. In 1937, the first Cotton Bowl Classic was played here. In 1960, the Dallas Texans (AFL) and the Dallas Cowboys (NFL) made their first season debut in the Cotton Bowl.

On February 10, 1942, a five-alarm blaze "raged unchecked for an hour in the automobile building." The damage was estimated at several hundred thousand dollars. One fireman was hospitalized after being overcome with smoke, and a half dozen others were given treatment at the scene. Roy Rupard, secretary of the State Fair Association, said that "the loss was covered by insurance."

Big Tex, a fifty-five-foot-tall cowboy statue, has been the symbol of the fair since his introduction in 1952. Where did Big Tex come from? In 1949, he was the world's largest Santa Claus in Kerens, Texas, about an hour south of Dallas. The town wanted to help attract Christmas shoppers, and Howell Brister had the idea to build a huge Santa. Everyone in the small town helped. Welders, garment factory workers and ranchers all did their part. The ranchers acted as models, and their body dimensions helped shape Big Santa (this would come in handy later). There was front-page newspaper coverage all over Texas. Big Santa was an instant celebrity.

However, by the next year (1950), the excitement had died down. Brister drove across the state trying to sell Big Santa. He approached the State Fair, and its organizers bought Santa in 1951 for $750. The State Fair's first thought was to just keep using him as Santa for the holidays. Then it came up with an idea: "Let's create a giant cowboy!" The fair hired Jack Bridges to make the alteration. Bridges was a very colorful and quirky artist. He gave Big Tex a bigger head and broader shoulders. The work went quickly (shaping the head in just three weeks). Big Tex was ready for opening day the following year.

In 1953, Big Tex's jaw was hinged so that he appears to be talking when announcements promote scheduled events. Jim Lowe was the voice of Big Tex for almost forty years. Many fairgoers give him credit for developing the Big Tex personality. Bill Bragg was the voice for another decade, but he had a falling out with the fair. The name of the current voice is a well-kept secret.

Elvis Presley performed at the Cotton Bowl during the 1956 season to a packed crowd.

In recent years, the fair has captured the nation's attention with its reputation as an event featuring unique foods. Fairgoers have been introduced to unusual deep-fried items, including Oreos, Twinkies, s'mores, pork ribs, cheesecake, butter, peanut butter and jelly and avocados. A batter-based fried Coke, chicken-fried bacon and fried banana splits have also been added to the bizarre diet at the annual September-October event.

In 2012, an electrical short in Big Tex's wiring sparked a fire. The flames inched up his body, eating away his clothes and his face within minutes. His charred steel frame stood for several hours as folks were crying, staring and taking pictures. The burnt giant cowboy was placed under a huge piece of canvas and was taken away from Big Tex Circle with a police escort.

Big Tex was rebuilt and reintroduced for the 2013 fair. Most folks in Texas believe that Big Tex is the world's tallest cowboy.

UFOS OVER EAST TEXAS

To a native Texan, our state is more than just "out of this world." And "The stars at night are big and bright, deep in the heart of Texas" is not just the beginning of our favorite song, but rather a foretelling of what is going on in our skies. Unidentified flying objects (UFOs) are being seen across Texas with increasing frequency. Our East Texas communities are no exception.

As early as 1897, there was a rash of sightings in the heart of East Texas. One possible explanation was that men working on the railroad made up stories at night and spread them to various stops the next day. One of those men, who testified publicly about what he saw, was a conductor known as "Truthful Skinny." He declared, "I saw a very small man repairing an airship in Wood County!"

The Texas skies in 1897 were "big and bright," and the event later called the Aurora Crash would become a local legend. Farmers in Wise County woke up on April 17 to find an article in their local newspaper titled "A Windmill Demolishes It." The story read:

> About 6 o'clock this morning the early risers of Aurora were astonished at the sudden appearance of the airship which has been sailing through the county. It was traveling due north, and much nearer the earth than ever before. Evidently, some of the machinery was out of order, for it was making a speed of only ten or twelve miles an hour and gradually settling toward the earth. It sailed directly over the public square, and when it reached the north part of town collided with the tower of Judge Proctor's windmill and went to pieces with a terrific explosion, scattering debris over several acres of ground, wrecking the windmill and water tank and destroying the Judge's flower garden.

The article went on to surmise:

> The pilot of the ship is supposed to have been the only one on board, and while his remains are badly disfigured, enough of the original has been picked up to show that he was not an inhabitant of this world. Papers found on his person—evidently the record of his travel—are written in some unknown hieroglyphics and cannot be deciphered.

The "pilot" (Orville and Wilbur Wright would not fly the first successful airship until six years later) was buried "with Christian rites" at the nearby Aurora Cemetery. (The cemetery contains a Texas Historical Commission marker mentioning the incident.) The Aurora Cemetery Association has denied all requests to exhume the site, and the grave marker has been removed that showed the exact location of the interment.

The Cash-Lundrum Incident near Huffman, Texas, in 1980 is the first UFO case where the witnesses sued the U.S. government for damages.

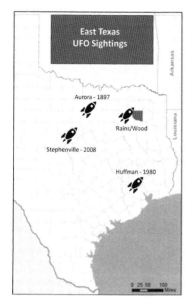

Location of UFOs seen in East Texas.
Author's graph.

Betty Cash, Vickie Landrum and her grandson Colby Landrum were driving from Huffman to Dayton when they came across a diamond-shaped craft hovering in the air shooting beams of fire at the ground. Betty left the vehicle and stood watching on the side of the road. To their utter surprise, the skies soon filled with helicopters. The helicopters appeared to be attempting to encircle and drive the UFO much like herding cattle.

When the three shocked participants finally arrived home, they all became very sick. The three witnesses were treated for radiation sickness and burns. Betty was admitted to a local hospital for fifteen days. The illnesses were considered life-threatening.

Later investigations could find no evidence linking the helicopters to any branch of the military. A Congressional hearing was held, but the government was not held responsible for any compensation.

Of all the UFO encounters in East Texas, no other case has had more eyewitnesses than the highly celebrated Stephenville Sightings, which occurred in and around the Erath County area in 2008. Reports of enormous spaceships moving over this area were made by some of the city's most esteemed citizens. Eyewitness reports, videos, photographs, drawings and sketches were handed over to the Mutual UFO Network (MUFON) when the group arrived for a full-fledged investigation in January 2008.

MUFON released a seventy-seven-page report on the sightings based on an analysis of radar records from the FAA and the National Weather Service, obtained through several FOIA requests, and comparing them to witness accounts. The report concluded that the radar data confirms the witness observations of an object, as well as the air force's statement that ten aircraft were operating in the area. It is too difficult to say for certain what the witnesses saw, but there was something there. Twice, they say, radar picked up an object traveling at nearly two thousand miles per hour, and at other times it showed a slow-moving object.

Recently, the National UFO Reporting Center ran a geospatial analysis on about thirty-eight thousand reports to identify the counties in Texas where most people claimed to have seen flying saucers. Rains County was ranked eighth, with 45.5 UFO sightings per capita.

In 2002, one report submitted to MUFON on Saturday, November 30, bluntly stated:

> *To anyone interested in UFO, or unidentified lights in the sky, the place to go is Rains County, Texas. My wife and I lived there for several years and have seen these lights on several occasions. We were once followed from our church by a mysterious light, and I actually stopped in the road, got out, and looked at it. It hovered behind us for several minutes, then moved off to the south slowly. We actually watched one from our front porch one evening, and I called the sheriff's department to see if they could identify it. They said that they could not.*

OLD RIP: EASTLAND COUNTY'S PRIDE AND JOY

"You're not going to believe this, but this story is true." At least, it is to the proud citizens of Eastland County, Texas.

The county seat is the town of Eastland, having been founded in 1858 and later organized in 1873. It is named for William Mosby Eastland, a soldier during the Texas Revolution and the only officer to die as a result of the "Black Bean executions" of the Mier expedition.

According to this local legend, when Eastland County's new courthouse was dedicated in 1897, several objects were placed in the cornerstone, including a Bible and other documents and proclamations. At the last minute, a justice of the peace walked up with a Texas horned lizard his son had caught that morning and placed it in the marble time capsule just before it was capped. The block was then sealed and placed at the corner of the town square. The courthouse went up around it, and the poor lizard was forgotten by most folks in the county.

Fast-forward thirty years. Progress and growth in Eastland required a larger public courthouse, and in 1928, the building was demolished to make way for a grand Art Deco courthouse on the same spot. Construction workers tore

Texas horned lizard (*Phrynosoma cornutum*). *Wikimedia Commons.*

down the walls, and when they got to the cornerstone, something miraculous occurred. They pried open the cornerstone including the time capsule, and a horned lizard peeked out. After three decades, the horny toad (as most Texans called them) was still alive!

Horned lizards (*Phrynosoma*) are a genus of North American lizards, of the family *Phrynosomatidae*. They are adapted to arid or semi-arid areas. Of the twenty-two species of horned lizards, fifteen are native to the United States. The largest-bodied and most widely distributed of the U.S. species is the Texas horned lizard. Most of this species only live a few years in the wild, so three decades encased in stone seemed impossible.

Folks in the county immediately named this freak of nature "Old Rip," after Rip Van Winkle. He was an instant celebrity in Eastland and surrounding counties, so much so that Will Wood, the man credited with catching the lizard as a boy, took Old Rip on tour across the country. The high point of the circuit was Old Rip getting to meet President Calvin Coolidge at the White House.

Then Old Rip became a regular on stage in downtown Dallas. This didn't sit well with his adoring fans in Eastland, and they talked Wood into bringing him back. Old Rip and Wood were hit with a lawsuit for an alleged breach of contract in Dallas, with damages accumulating to more than $6,000. The famed horny toad was seized by officials in Dallas and ended up in county jail before heading home to Eastland.

Rip Van Winkle didn't live forever, and neither did Old Rip. He died about a year later in his home (a fishbowl filled with sand and red ants for snacks). The papers reported that it was probably pneumonia.

This was not, however, the end of Old Rip. By this time, the world-renowned Texas horned lizard was so important to Eastland that he was embalmed and placed in a velvet-lined casket. He was placed on display in the lobby of the new Eastland County Courthouse, where tourists could pay their respects. Even John Connally stopped by while running for governor of Texas in 1962 for a photo op. Connally lifted the embalmed creature by its hind leg, which promptly popped off.

Eastland hosts Ripfest the first Saturday in October each year to honor its most famous resident. This year, the festival included a 5K race, a large parade, vendor booths, bounce houses, pony rides, a car show and tons of food.

The Texas horned lizards' round, flat bodies and namesake horns make them look prehistoric. Their unique defense mechanism of shooting blood from their eyes at canine predators only adds to their reputation as Texas tough. The Comanche people believed that these creatures would always run in the direction of bison and used them to guide hunts. Other American Indian cultures saw them as symbols of strength. Cowboys on cattle drives told stories of horny toads that could live a century or more.

Unfortunately, these days the Texas horned lizard (the official state reptile) is in dire straits. For several decades, they've been vanishing from Texas landscapes for reasons researchers cannot fully determine. Jaimie Peltier, a zookeeper at the Fort Worth Zoo, explained:

> *The horned lizard is not on the brink of extinction—yet. It is listed as "threatened" in the state, but strong populations in New Mexico and elsewhere keep it off the federal endangered species list. Status as a state treasure helps give the lizard cultural protection, but it could easily become just another Texas legend.*

When I was a young knucklehead in the '50s, my dad worked for a company headquartered in Pennsylvania. When officials came to East Texas to make inspections, I would catch as many horny toads as I could get my hands on and sell them to the northerners for twenty-five cents each. I just hope I didn't contribute to the decline of the species by selling one of Old Rip's kinfolk!

Part III

1900—1950

The 1907 Shoot-Out in Winnsboro, Texas

Winnsboro, Texas, known as the "Crossroads of East Texas," is a quiet community that treasures its past but embraces the tourist trade with its unique shops and eateries. If you have visited lately, you can't help but notice the town's makeover. Many of the buildings got a facelift when Winnsboro became a Texas Main Street City in the Texas Historical Commission's "downtown revitalization program." With the state pouring in $12 million, spruced-up storefronts, reworked streets and sidewalks and replica lighting offer a fresh yet nostalgic ambiance for the thriving tourist market.

The town, first settled in the early 1850s, was named for John E. Wynn, an Englishman who settled in the area. Originally spelled Wynnsborough, it was changed to Winnsborough when a post office was established in 1855. By 1861, in addition to the post office, the community had two general stores and a church. In 1876, the East Line and Red River Railroad built a narrow-gauge road west from Jefferson, and the town developed into an important local shipping center. The town's name was shortened to Winnsboro in 1893, evidently at the request of city leaders.

In 1904, the Texas Southern Railroad built through the town, and soon the flourishing community had four banks, two potteries, a public library, a cottonseed mill, two weekly newspapers (the *Wide Awake* and the *Wortham Messenger*) and a population of 2,300. Home to thousands of acres of longleaf

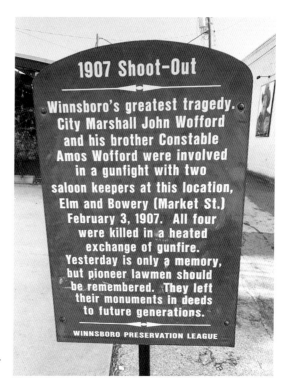

Winnsboro Preservation League marker depicting the 1907 shoot-out. *Author's collection.*

yellow pine trees and hardwood timber, Winnsboro attracted many sawmills and loggers. With the expansion of the railroad and the relative ease of shipping and receiving, the timber industry was booming. At the peak of the timber cutting business, thirty sawmills with spirited loggers looking for entertainment populated the area.

The alley street north of the depot became known as the "Bowery," complete with saloons, gambling halls and bathhouses that catered to the loggers. Not surprisingly, with that type of atmosphere, Winnsboro also had its share of gunplay, as indicated by the marker placed in the exact location of one such shoot-out in 1907.

The Winnsboro Preservation League may have gotten the exact spot correct, but there is some dispute as to the date. Most historical accounts have the date as February 2, 1907, which was a Saturday. Saturday night is a more likely candidate for a gunfight in a drinking establishment than a Sunday night in the "Bible Belt" of East Texas.

The Wofford brothers—Amos R., Wood County deputy sheriff, and John S., Wood County Precinct 3 constable—were on routine patrol of the Bowery just prior to the usual Saturday night drinking and partying.

Amos was born on September 5, 1871, and was thirty-five years of age on this fateful Saturday night. He was previously a city marshal. John was thirty-two years of age, having been born on February 26, 1874.

R.O. "Dick" Milam, age fifty, was the proprietor of an illegal liquor operation known as a "blind tiger." Helping him that evening was his twenty-three-year-old son, W.W. "Bud" Milam, a Dallas fireman.

At about 5:30 p.m., an altercation occurred on Elm Street. It is unknown what exactly preceded the incident, but it is believed that the Woffords intended to arrest the Milams for liquor violations. One of the Milams produced a handgun and opened fire. Both Woffords were hit but managed to return fire. When the smoke cleared, all four men were on the ground. Dick Milam died at the scene. Amos and John Wofford both died two days later on February 4, 1907. Bud Milam died on February 11, 1907.

Amos Richard Wofford had been with the Wood County Sheriff's Office for ten years. He was survived by his wife, Sally Dea Tramel, and three children. He is buried at the Union Cemetery near Sulphur Springs. He was a member of the Woodsmen of the World, as indicated by his marker.

John S. Wofford was survived by his wife, Dove, and two children. He is buried at the Shooks Chapel Cemetery in rural Hopkins County, Texas. John had chosen law enforcement to follow in his brother's footsteps.

Dick Milam and Bud Milam are buried at the Hopewell Cemetery, southwest of Winnsboro. Dick had been born in Alabama, but Bud was born in Texas. In a strange twist of fate, Bud was also a member of the Woodsmen of the World.

Four dead in one gunfight. It would tragically change the lives of these families, but their names live on in the historic section of the Bowery, as shoppers, diners and tourists stop to read the marker, enlightening us to the tale of the 1907 shoot-out.

GOT MILK?

As I drive to the Yantis Café each morning for breakfast, I am always in awe of the dairy cattle in the fields along the way and the hustle and bustle involved with their daily care. They have to be fed (no matter how cold it is) and they have to be milked (no matter how early it is), and I know that someone has to do it or I won't get my cold, foamy glass of Grade A pasteurized homogenized milk. I'm just thankful it's not me!

When the first Texans settled the country, native cattle stemmed from Spanish or Mexican roots, and Longhorns were known as "exceedingly poor milkers." In 1880, the first purebred Jerseys were imported, and in 1884, the first purebred Holstein calves were born in the state. These became the two main breeds in Texas's dairy history. Jerseys would become the most popular dairy breed because, until the mid-1900s, most milk was marketed as cream, butter or cheese rather than as whole milk. Jersey produced milk with the highest butterfat content. By 1949, 75 percent of the estimated 1,283,000 milk cows in Texas were Jerseys.

The stock market crash of 1929, which didn't affect East Texas until 1930–31, had an impact on all farming and ranching. The number of farms in Hopkins County fell from 5,005 in 1930 to 4,324 in 1940, a decrease of 13.6 percent. Many of the tenant farmers left the land, and by 1940, tenantry had declined to less than 50 percent of the farmers in the county. Unemployment, recorded at 1.5 percent in 1930, rose to 15 percent by 1940.

The Texas longhorn is a beautiful animal but not much good for milking. *Wikimedia Commons.*

As late as 1935, relief figures for Hopkins County showed 2,626 workers on some sort of relief program.

Even in these bad times, Hopkins County dairies were saved by a project begun in 1929 that would have far-reaching effects. That year, voters approved a bond package to finance paved roads throughout the county to secure a milk processing plant for Sulphur Springs. In 1935, most of the work was completed, and in 1937, the Carnation Milk Company opened a processing plant. This plant paved the way for large-scale dairy farming.

Dairy farming quickly surpassed all other types of farming in the county in importance and income. From 1936 to 1949, some two hundred class-A dairies were established in the county. The number of cattle grew from 25,086 in 1930 to 34,920 in 1940, an increase of 39 percent.

The Texas Agricultural Extension Service released figures in 1950 stating that on a cow-per-acre basis, Hopkins had become the leading county in milk production in the state, with almost five hundred dairies producing 17 percent of the state total. Hopkins County was recognized as the "Dairy Capital of Texas" and remained so until about 1990.

In the 1980s, milk production was still centered on the eastern part of the state. More than 90 percent was produced east of a line from Wichita Falls to Brownwood to San Antonio to Corpus Christi. Urban counties no longer led in milk production. Until the 1950s, Harris, Dallas, Tarrant and Bexar Counties usually led as milk producers. In the 1980s, Hopkins, Erath and Wise Counties were the new leaders. These three counties accounted for about 30 percent of the state's product, and Hopkins County alone produced 16 percent of the Texas total. Texas generally ranked in the top ten states of the nation in milk production during the 1970s and 1980s, and Texas farmers received a gross income of $504,583,000 from milk in 1980.

According to the Texas A&M AgriLife Extension office in Sulphur Springs, there are currently only sixty-five dairies in Hopkins County. What happened? Bobby Wayne Ogle, a dairyman for forty-four years in the Yantis area, smiled when asked the question. "There have been a lot of different reasons for the dairy industry's decline since the early '90s, but it wasn't blackleg or bluetongue disease that caused the decline. It was most likely a special kind of foot and mouth disease…called 'government regulation!'"

Shortly after Lake Fork was impounded, the Environmental Protection Agency (EPA) took great interest in "what was running into the waters" from the surrounding farms and ranches. New regulations concerning runoff made it financially improbable for small dairy owners to pay for the required renovations and make a profit at the same time. Many owners with fewer than one hundred cows found other occupations to meet their families' needs.

Bobby and his family hung in there. "In those days, if your wife and family weren't willing to pitch in where needed, you didn't make it in the dairy business," he explained. "The work is hard and relentless, but it builds a strong cohesive family and prepares your children for the challenges ahead when they have their own families."

"It didn't hurt that my wife's family had also been in the dairy business for the last four generations and she knew what to expect," Bobby added. "Producing milk is not just milking cows—you have to have good financial management, and Carolyn is the best. Our youngest son, Tanner, has now taken over the business and is continuing the legacy of a family farm."

"There were other factors that led to dairy production leaving Hopkins County," Bobby continued. "The state gave special incentives to foreign entities [low interest rates and five-year tax deferments] to move to Texas and open dairies. These people paid too much for dairy cows [low interest], driving up cattle prices, and in five years they packed up and returned to their native countries. But they narrowed the competition, as many concerns couldn't compete."

Even new technology contributed. "When new drugs were invented to increase a cow's production, everyone wanted them of course, but more production with the same demand from the consumers led to falling milk prices. When the milk prices fall, but the feed prices stay the same or go up, you are soon out of business!"

When asked about the future of the dairy business in the area, Bobby was quick to point out, "Children today have so many opportunities that were not available to us in the late '60s. I don't see many second- or third-generation small dairy families in the future. Only the large conglomerates with thousands of cows will be able to compete in the marketplace."

One result of the decline in the family dairy farm is the advent of the specialty or "boutique" dairy. The Waldo Way Dairy Farm, located just off Highway 37 between Quitman and Mineola, is one such enterprise. Owned and operated by Dr. NaRisha (Ris) Waldo and her son, Trenton Montgomery, the dairy store serves customers throughout East Texas.

The Waldo Way is the first robotic dairy farm in the state. This robot (an Astrea 20/20) allows the cows to be milked at any time of the day. All the cows are named, tagged and chipped. The robot scans the chip when the cow enters, takes its vital signs, tests the quality of the milk and sends an e-mail or text to management. It takes about two days for a new cow to learn to enter the milking chute without encouragement. With a robotic operation, cows can be milked without a human presence. The cows are registered with the American Guernsey Association, and the Waldo Way is the only registered 100 percent Guernsey grade-A raw milk dairy in the state.

Opening in 2013, this boutique dairy store was an immediate success, selling out of milk the first day. In addition to the raw Guernsey milk, dairy products include buttermilk, drinkable yogurt, cheese, cream and butter. The farm store also sells natural food products from other farmers, such as bread, meats, jam and honey.

In summing up the Waldo Way experience, Dr. Waldo explained:

> *I look at my registered Guernseys as my partners, if you will, on this farm adventure. The milk is sweet, the yogurt is creamy, the hand-churned butter looks like a pot of gold and of course, there is always "Mom's Cheese" in my very own seasonal varieties. Visitors add life, depth, character and are a pleasure to have on the farm. Bring the children, see the beautiful Guernsey cow and savor the gold milk. It is our pleasure to welcome you to our farm.*

The Last Muster

June 27—The opening session of the Hood's Texas Brigade Association was called to order at 9:30 a.m. this morning, with Miss Katie Daffan, life secretary of Hood's Brigade (and the only female member) presiding. The headline in the *Bryan Daily Eagle* would read, "1934 Reunion, Bryan TX—Survivors of Confederacy in Reunion."

The brigade, later to be nicknamed "Hood's Texas Brigade," was originally organized on October 22, 1861, in Richmond, Virginia. It was initially commanded by Brigadier General Louis T. Wigfall and composed of the First, Fourth and Fifth Texas Infantry Regiments. The Fourth Texas was commanded by Colonel John Bell Hood of Owingsville, Kentucky. On March 7, 1862, Hood was promoted to brigadier general and placed in command. Hood's brigade served throughout the Civil War in James Longstreet's First Corps of Robert E. Lee's Army of Northern Virginia. It participated in at least twenty-four battles in 1862, including Eltham's Landing, Gaines's Mill, Second Manassas and Sharpsburg (Antietam).

Confederate general John Bell Hood, namesake of the Hood's Texas Brigade Association. *Wikimedia Commons.*

The year 1863 brought the battles at Gettysburg and Chickamauga, where Hood was wounded. He was forced to leave his division, ending his official connection with the brigade. His "boys" would go on to fight at the Sieges of Chattanooga and Knoxville and the Battle of the Wilderness before surrendering with Lee at Appomattox on April 10, 1865.

Estimates by historians put the strength of the Texas regiments at about 3,500 men at the beginning of the Civil War. During the war, recruits increased the number to almost 4,400. The "boys from Texas" sustained a 61 percent casualty rate and, at its surrender, numbered only 600 officers and men.

The local Bryan paper dutifully reported on each of the annual reunions held in the town. The record of these assemblies stands as a testament to the resourcefulness, loyalty and camaraderie of these forgotten warriors. Miss Daffan routinely read the list of those who had "passed over the river to be with Lee and Jackson" on each occasion, but much of the news carried a hopeful tone. In 1927, it was reported that Captain E.W.B. Leach has stopped over in Austin at the Confederate Home in route to the reunion and witnessed the marriage of R.P.H. Calhoun, age ninety-two, and Annie Elizabeth Pollard, age eighty-one. "The couple left immediately on a honeymoon trip to San Antonio," Captain Leach said.

Entertainment was usually a significant part of the agenda. The 1928 reunion included a song by Mrs. H.C. Wright of Austin, described as being past eighty years of age and "yet has a wonderful sweet voice." Mrs. E. Davis of Houston, the mother of Dick Dowling Camp, challenged Colonel James Briggs to a "buck and wing" contest, and Mrs. A.J. Buchanan played the piano while two young chaps virtually brought down the house as they danced to "Turkey in the Straw."

The attendees traveling to Bryan for the meetings were not just soldiers. On more than one occasion, Frank Simms, an eighty-five-year-old former slave and Colonel Hood's cook during the war, was recognized in the official record. It was noted that he said he considers Democrats to be the bravest men in the world and Baptists to be the best Christians—but he went on to say that he remains a Baptist but is about persuaded to quit the Democrats!

Sometimes during the meetings, the news was all too familiar to the dwindling brigade that had known so much bad news and death during the war. R.H. Kirk, age eighty-three, of Houston, died at ten o'clock on the second day of the meeting in 1930 at the home of his relatives, Mr. and Mrs. C.S. LaHatte, 3010 South College Avenue, Bryan.

On this morning in 1934, Miss Daffan waited around in the meeting room in the hotel for the old soldiers to arrive. None did—the handful that had traveled to the reunion were too feeble to come downstairs in the hotel to the meeting. Katie slowly, solemnly called the roll, pausing after each name to listen carefully for a response. There was none. When she reached the end of the roll, with no response, she formally adjourned the meeting and closed the books on the Hood's Texas Brigade Association. It would be the last muster.

Reo Palm Isle: An East Texas Legend

When Elvis Aaron Presley took the stage at the Reo Palm Isle Club on January 27, 1955, not many East Texans were familiar with him or his style. The club's co-owner, Glynn Keeling, would later recall, "Nobody knew who

Elvis was. He'd get up there and jump around, and all these old cronies, like me, they didn't have no idea what he was doing." East Texans may not have heard of Elvis yet, but they had been flocking to this club since 1935.

The Palm Isle Amusement Corporation—formed by George L. Culver, A.G. Carter, Tom Cook and E.B. (Bill) Deane—wanted to build a place that would be "the largest and most elaborate night club in the South." Using Texas ingenuity and a $20,000 bankroll, they constructed an 80-by-180-foot building at the intersection of Farm Road 1845 and Highway 31 in Longview, Texas. Longview, settled in the 1880s, got its name after surveyors working on the Texas and Pacific Railroad were astonished at the "long distant view" from the townsite. Apparently, these Texas entrepreneurs had a long-distant view as well, considering the legendary status the club has since achieved.

They used the finest hardwoods available in 1935 to construct the dance floor, which could easily accommodate 1,500 couples with five square feet allotted per person. Any large band would find room on the twenty-by-thirty-foot stage. Customer tables were lined on a spacious raised floor to not interfere with the dancers. Opening night on Thursday, September 12, the club, now named Palm Isle, produced a capacity crowd of more than three thousand patrons! Eddy Duchin and the New York Central Park Casino

Reo Palm Isle sign in Longview, Texas. *Author's collection.*

Orchestra performed. "I Only Have Eyes for You" was a recent hit single for the band, and the crowd danced until closing time.

It wasn't long before couples were coming from as far away as Chicago and New York to listen and dance to the "big bands" of the time. The likes of Glenn Miller, Tommy Dorsey, Ted Lewis, Ozzie Nelson, Ella Fitzgerald, Jack Teagarden, Louis Armstrong, Paul Whiteman, Jan Garber, Gene Krupa, Glen Gray and Herb Cook all frequented the ballroom during this era. Imagine going to see Tommy Dorsey and hearing the young singer Frank Sinatra crooning "Stardust."

Between 1935 and 1951, the club changed owners and names several times. New owners included Hal Cooper, Mattie Castleberry and Jack and Neva Starnes (Neva's Palm Isle). In December 1951, Sherman Sparks, along with his partner Glynn Keeling, purchased the Palm Isle from Mattie Castleberry. Because Sparks had previously owned a small club named the Reo in Kilgore (it burned down), he renamed the venue the Reo Palm Isle. In July 1956, Sparks sold his ownership in the club to Glynn Keeling.

The Reo Palm Isle was not the only place in East Texas that Elvis and his fellow entertainers from the "Louisiana Hayride" performed. Singing his hit "Blue Moon of Kentucky" had made Elvis popular in the area. He appeared at Kilgore's Driller Park, Gladewater's high school and old Bear Stadium and in shows at Gilmer, Tyler, Gaston, DeKalb, Carthage, Paris and Henderson.

Gladewater radio station KSIJ had a major hand in spreading the word about artists and dates performing in the Piney Woods. The AM station was located on the top floor of T.W. Lee's four-story building on U.S. 80. "Gentleman" Jim Reeves and Tom Perryman were among the station's deejays. Perryman (now a member of the National Disc Jockey Hall of Fame) was a "Hayride" promoter and served as the master of ceremonies when Presley came to the Reo Palm Isle in 1955 with Jim Ed and Maxine Brown. "I probably was the only hillbilly disc jockey playing Elvis's record," Perryman said.

Gladewater's role in rock history includes more than Elvis. Also in 1955, a young Johnny Cash played a show there with the great Carl Perkins, author of "Blue Suede Shoes." Sitting in the dressing room waiting to go on stage, Cash penned a tune that became one of his biggest hits. "I Walk the Line" would become a number one country hit!

On August 15, 1955, just four days after playing the Reo Palm Isle, Elvis signed a management contract with Colonel Tom Parker. By the next year, the former Memphis truck driver was no longer playing the Reo Palm Isle, any of the East Texas venues or any VFW halls, high school gyms or ribbon-cuttings. Elvis had made it to the "big time."

By the 1970s, the Reo Palm Isle had focused mainly on country and western music. These performances have included such artists as Jim Reeves, Ray Price, Waylon Jennings, David Frizzell, Boots Randolph, Loretta Lynn, Shelly West, Jerry Lee Lewis, Frenchie Burke, Willie Nelson, Joe Stampley, Jacky Ward, Johnny Paycheck, Boxcar Willie, Hank Williams Jr., Ronnie Milsap, Lee Greenwood, Ricky Skaggs, Delbert McClinton, David Allan Coe and Mickey Gilley.

In 1975, the Associated Press named the Reo Palm Isle the "Best Club" in Texas, and in 1976, *Texas Monthly* magazine named it "Dance Hall of the Year."

Wouldn't it be something to tell your grandchildren that you saw Willie Nelson at the Reo. Or, even better, to tell them that your grandfather saw Frank Sinatra and your father saw Elvis at the Reo Palm Isle in Longview, Texas!

BARROW GANG SURVIVOR: THE SURPRISING STORY OF BENNIE IVA CALDWELL

Bennie Iva Caldwell was born in Garvin, Oklahoma, on New Year's Day in 1811, the only child of Matthew Fontain Caldwell and Lillian Bell Pond. Her mother was only fifteen years old at the time of her birth. Fontain, age thirty-nine, and Lillian divorced while Bennie was still a young child. A devoutly religious man, he raised her by himself. His occupation was logger and farmer, but he occasionally preached as a lay minister.

At age seventeen, now called Blanche, her mother (although still estranged) arranged for her to be married to John Calloway, a much older man. Blanche would later say that the experience with Calloway left her unable to bear children.

While hiding in Dallas County from her husband, John, Blanche met Marvin "Buck" Barrow on November 11, 1929. Buck was a twice-divorced criminal with children from a previous marriage and eight years her senior. Several days later, Barrow was shot and captured following a burglary in Denton. He was sentenced to five years in the Texas State Prison System.

On March 8, 1930, Buck escaped from the Ferguson Prison Farm near Midway, Texas. Authorities would later learn that Blanche not only knew of

Blanche Barrow being taken into custody near Dexter, Iowa. *Wikimedia Commons.*

his escape but also accompanied him on his getaway. While on the run, they married in Oklahoma on July 2, 1931, and honeymooned in Florida.

It didn't take long for Blanche to realize that it wasn't going to work out with Buck still being a fugitive. She convinced him to turn himself in. Two years later, the then governor of Texas, "Ma" Ferguson, had Buck paroled. It was only a few days later that Buck and Blanche were paid a visit by Buck's brother, Clyde, and his girlfriend, Bonnie Parker. Little brother convinced Buck to vacation with them in Joplin, Missouri, in August 1933.

In Joplin, when confronted, Buck and Clyde shot and killed two police officers. While fleeing law enforcement not far from Dexter, Iowa, the Barrow Gang was caught in an ambush. A bloody gun battle broke out, and Buck was shot four times in the back. Blanche and Buck became separated from the others, and he collapsed. When the shooting continued and Buck was again wounded, they stood up and surrendered. A famous photo shows a distraught Blanche moments after she was pulled away from Buck, who is lying mortally wounded yards to her right. Blanche was shot in the face, blinding her in her left eye. Bonnie and Clyde, however, once again slipped away from the grasp of the law.

Blanche was taken into custody and extradited to Missouri, where she was charged with "Assault with Intent to Kill." She was sentenced to ten years. Her sentence was commuted, and she was released from Missouri State Penitentiary in Kansas City after serving just over five and a half years. Blanche took a train from Union Station in Kansas City back home to Garvin, Oklahoma.

There were no jobs in Garvin, so Blanche moved to Dallas. She went to work as a waitress at the Interurban Café. The Dallas Interurban was a transit system, running trains to Waco and Sherman and a trolley near downtown. The café was in the main terminal building. In 1940, she met and married Eddie Frasure and completed the terms of her parole one year later.

By 1951, they were living in Pleasant Grove and had joined a church, and Blanche was teaching Sunday school. Once while on the run with Buck, desperately needing some comfort from the Lord, she stole a Bible. Now Blanche was able to give every graduating student in her Sunday school class a Bible so they wouldn't have to steal one.

In the mid-1960s, Blanche, now Mrs. Frasure, was approached by the actor Warren Beatty, who wanted to purchase the right to use her name in a new film called *Bonnie and Clyde*. After reading the script for accuracy, she agreed. After the movie was released, she realized that the script had been changed, and she now believed her portrayal by Estelle Parsons was unrealistic. On April 10, 1968, at the Fortieth Academy Awards ceremony, Parsons won the Academy Award for Best Supporting Actress. Blanche's response was brief and to the point: "That movie made me look like a screaming horse's ass."

Although Blanche hated the movie, she really liked Warren Beatty. When they had off-time during the location filming, he would stop by and visit with her. She enjoyed listening to Warren play tunes on her piano.

Even as late as the '70s, federal, state and local law enforcement agencies continued to keep tabs on the former Barrow Gang survivor. Blanche had contended that during one interrogation, J. Edgar Hoover had threated to gouge out her one remaining good eye. She did, however, believe that the man who arrested her for attempted murder in 1933, Sheriff Holt Coffey, was remarkably fair and sympathetic.

Bennie Ivy Caldwell-Calloway-Barrow-Frasure died from cancer at age seventy-seven in 1988. She was survived by her ninety-three-year-old mother. She is buried at Dallas's Grove Hill Memorial Park under the name Blanche B. Frasure. Her memoir, *My Life with Bonnie and Clyde*, was published in 2004, many years after her death.

Texas Sports Star's Last Full Measure of Devotion

Andrew Jackson Lummus Jr. was born on October 22, 1915, on a cotton farm in Ellis County near Ennis, Texas. By the time he started high school in Ennis in

September 1931, the Great Depression was taking its toll on all the farmers in East Texas. Jack, as his classmates called him, dropped out of school his senior year because, in the view of his family, buying a picture and a gown was wasteful during such dire times.

He would finish his high school education at Texas Military College, receiving a two-year sports scholarship and winning all-conference honors in football. Baylor and Tulane University came calling, and Jack enrolled at Baylor in September 1937. At Baylor, Jack was honorable mention All-American in football and All–Southwest Conference in baseball. Teammates have said he was probably better at baseball than football, having batted .320 for the

Jack Lummus, USMC, Medal of Honor recipient, awarded posthumously. *Wikimedia Commons.*

Bears. His coach once told a reporter, "Lummus was the best centerfielder in the history of Baylor or anywhere else." Before he left Baylor, Jack signed a minor-league baseball contract with the Wichita Falls Spudders and a uniform player's contract with the New York Giants in the NFL.

Lummus played twenty-six games for the Spudders in right and center field and had a .257 batting average. Jack then reported to Hicks Field, forty miles northwest of Fort Worth, to honor a commitment he had made at Baylor to serve in the U.S. Army Air Corps. Unfortunately, while taxiing on the runway after making his first solo flight, he accidentally clipped a fence with his wingtip and washed out of flight school.

The next stop for Jack was the New York Giants football team. He signed as a free agent, was paid $100 per game and played in nine games. On December 7, 1941, the Giants were playing their archrivals, the Brooklyn Dodgers, when at halftime the Associated Press ticker in the press box read, "Airplanes identified as Japanese have attacked the American Naval Base at Pearl Harbor!"

After joining the U.S. Marine Corps, Jack received a commission as a second lieutenant after completing the Officer's Training School at Quantico, Virginia. First Lieutenant Jack Lummus was in the first wave of troops to land at Iwo Jima on February 19, 1945. Jack and his platoon landed at 9:00 a.m. on the beach known as "Red One." This would be his last landing with his brothers. His Medal of Honor citation reads as follows:

For conspicuous gallantry and intrepidity at the risk of his life above and beyond the call of duty as leader of a Rifle Platoon attached to the 2d Battalion, 27th Marines, 5th Marine Division, in action against enemy Japanese forces on Iwo Jima in the Volcano Islands, 8 March 1945. Resuming his assault tactics with a bold decision after fighting without respite for 2 days and nights, 1st Lt. Lummus slowly advanced his platoon against an enemy deeply entrenched in a network of mutually supporting positions. Suddenly halted by a terrific concentration of hostile fire, he unhesitatingly moved forward of his front lines in an effort to neutralize the Japanese position. Although knocked to the ground when an enemy grenade exploded close by, he immediately recovered himself and, again moving forward despite the intensified barrage, quickly located, attacked, and destroyed the occupied emplacement. Instantly taken under fire by the garrison of a supporting pillbox and further assailed by the slashing fury of hostile rifle fire, he fell under the impact of a second enemy grenade but, courageously disregarding painful shoulder wounds, staunchly continued his heroic 1-man assault and charged the second pillbox, annihilating all the occupants. Subsequently returning to his platoon position, he fearlessly traversed his lines under fire, encouraging his men to advance and directing the fire of supporting tanks against other stubbornly holding Japanese emplacements. Held up again by a devastating barrage, he again moved into the open, rushed a third heavily fortified installation and killed the defending troops. Determined to crush all resistance, he led his men indomitably, personally attacking foxholes and spider traps with his carbine and systematically reducing the fanatic opposition until, stepping on a land mine, he sustained fatal wounds. By his outstanding valor, skilled tactics, and tenacious perseverance in the face of overwhelming odds, 1st Lt. Lummus had inspired his stouthearted marines to continue the relentless drive northward, thereby contributing materially to the success of his regimental mission. His dauntless leadership and unwavering devotion to duty throughout sustain and enhance the highest traditions of the U.S. Naval Service. He gallantly gave his life in the service of his country.

When Jack was removed from the field with no legs and carried to the aid station, his last words were, "Well, Doc, the New York Giants lost a mighty good end today."

The family couldn't afford a trip to Washington, D.C., for the ceremonies, so Rear Admiral Joseph Clark presented Laura Lummus her son's Medal of Honor in a memorial service at the Tabernacle Baptist Church in Ennis on May 30, 1946. On April 20, 1948, Lummus was reburied at the Myrtle Cemetery in Ennis.

Jack Lummus was one of the twenty-seven marines awarded the Medal of Honor for his heroics on Iwo Jima. The U.S. Navy honored our Texas hero with the naming of a new maritime prepositioning ship, the USNS *1ˢᵗ LT Jack Lummus*, in 1986. The City of Ennis, Texas, dedicated Jack Lummus Memorial Park in December of that year, and the Jack Lummus Intermediate School is also named in his honor.

Although his sports career is what legends are made from, Andrew Jackson Lummus Jr. viewed his service to his country in time of war as more important than any athletic accomplishment. Lummus was one of only two players (along with former Detroit Lion Maurice Britt of Arkansas) from the National Football League to receive the Medal of Honor. The New York Giants erected a plaque honoring Lummus in December 1945. A memorial exhibit containing his original Medal of Honor citation is on display at Baylor University. On October 11, 2015, the New York Giants inducted Lummus into the "Ring of Honor" at Metlife Stadium.

SISSY SPACEK: QUITMAN LIVING LEGEND

Mary Elizabeth Spacek was born on December 25, 1949, in Quitman, Texas. Her mother, Virginia Frances Spilman, who was of Polish, English and Irish descent, was from the Rio Grande Valley. Her father, Edwin Arnold Spacek Sr. (from a long line of Czech farmers), was the local county agricultural agent. From birth, her brothers always called her Sissy, which led to her taking this nickname as her stage name when the bright lights of Hollywood outgrew the warm lights of East Texas.

In 1991, as Sissy related to *Texas Monthly*:

> *When she was six years old, she and her family went to a one-room school-house in nearby Coke (population: 25) and watched the Cokettes march across the stage and twirl their batons. The Cokettes wore silver cowgirl outfits and white boots. It was the first time in Sissy's life that she felt the urge to perform. There was something magical happening on that stage, and she wanted to be part of it. "I remember sitting there in the audience,*

wanting more than anything in the world to be a Cokette," says Sissy. Not a movie star, but a Cokette.

"I had an epiphany as a child," said Spacek in another magazine article, one of the hundreds that have been written about her career. "My brother and I must have been six or seven years old. We were barefoot; it was the summer. We went with my mother to an African American lady's home who did upholstery, and we stayed outside and played with her two children while our mothers were indoors, discussing this upholstery work." This was the age of polio, when every parent cautioned their children not to drink after someone else, not even brothers or sisters:

> *It was a hot, hot day, and we all jumped up on this well in their yard.... The boy pulled up a bucket and a metal cup and took a sip and started passing it around. I remember looking at this water and thinking, "I know I'm not supposed to do this. And when I put that cup to my lips, it was the coolest, sweetest water I'd ever had."*

Fear was something she would not let stop her from following her dreams.

Tragedy struck the Spacek family in 1967. Her brother, Robbie, died from leukemia after a short illness. She told the *Toronto Star* that it was "the defining event of my whole life." She used this personal tragedy as a tool to be fearless in her acting career. "I think it made me brave. Once you experience something like that, you've experienced the ultimate tragedy."

After graduating from Quitman High School and serving as Homecoming Queen her senior year, Sissy enrolled in Lee Strasberg's Actors Studio (with the help of her first cousin, actor Rip Torn) and then the Lee Strasberg Institute in New York. "Never think you're better than anyone else, but don't let anyone treat you like you're worse than they are," was Rip's advice.

The acting lessons were successful, and her first credited role was in the 1972 cult

Mary Elizabeth (Sissy) Spacek made her first movie right out of high school. *Wikimedia Commons.*

classic *Prime Cut* (starring Lee Marvin and Gene Hackman), in which she played Poppy, a girl sold into sexual slavery. The good folks in Quitman would learn just how "fearless" Sissy had become when they saw her in this film totally nude.

Sissy has appeared in more than forty movies and numerous television shows and has recorded five music singles. She is a six-time Academy Award nominee, winning once for *Coal Miner's Daughter* (1980). She has also won three Golden Globe Awards, for *Coal Miner's Daughter*, *Crimes of the Heart* (1986) and *In the Bedroom* (2001).

In 2012, Sissy Spacek published a memoir, *My Extraordinary Ordinary Life*, with coauthor Maryanne Vollers. The book is about what matters most: the exquisite worth of ordinary things, the simple pleasures of home and family and the honest job of being right with the world. "If I get hit by a truck tomorrow," she wrote, "I want to know I've returned my neighbor's cake pan."

PART IV

SINCE 1950

ESSENCE OF THE TEXAS SPIRIT:
THE LEGACY OF *HOME FROM THE HILL*

"Home is the sailor, home from sea, And the hunter home from the hill." This is the defining poetic line by Robert Louis Stevenson that opens the 1960 classic Texas movie *Home from the Hill*.

The book of the same name was written two years earlier by William Humphrey (his first novel) about his hometown, Clarksville, Texas. He would go on to write thirteen books, and his work was reviewed by the *New York Times* as "[f]unny, vivid and moving, this is a fine piece of work and a delight to read." Unlike the movie *Home for the Hill*, the novel begins with the funeral of "Miz Hannah" Hunnicutt in her East Texas hometown a dozen years after her commitment to a Dallas asylum. Her burial between the tombs of her husband, Wade, and her son, Theron, is the final episode of Clarksville folklore that unfolds within this powerful Texas tale.

It is the tragic events surrounding the murder of Hannah's authoritative and charismatic husband and the subsequent attempt at revenge by their son that make this story memorable. Theron, their only child, was intensely affected by the volatile relationship between his brooding mother and his wayward father. The emulation of his father's impetuous, self-destructive behavior not only unnerved his mother but also became the impetus for his involvement with the pretty Libby Halstead. This first love and her incensed

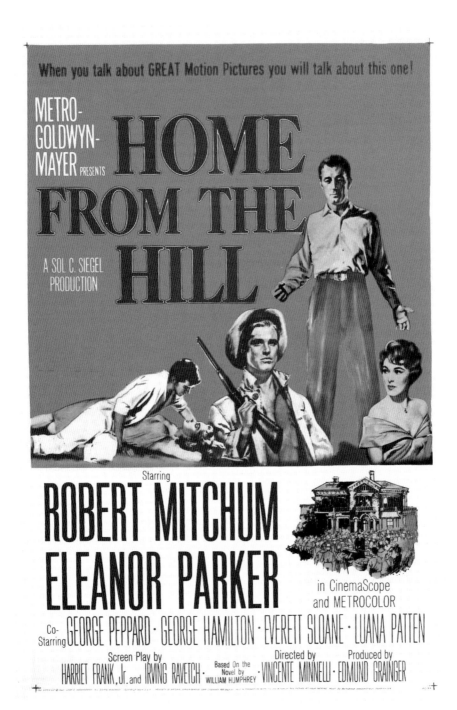

Theatrical release poster for the movie *Home from the Hill*. *Wikimedia Commons.*

father's vengeful reaction propelled this devastating saga to its shattering, inevitable conclusion.

Metro-Goldwyn-Mayer picked up the movie rights to Humphrey's larger-than-life Texas saga and began filming in Oxford, Mississippi, near the University of Mississippi campus. However, this movie could not have been as authentic without filming most of the location scenes in the author's hometown and nearby Paris, Texas. The homes used in the movie, particularly the interior shots, are in Clarksville, as are the "downtown" shots along the streets in this Northeast Texas small town. Some hunting scenes were filmed near Lake Crook. Other scenes, including at "Sulfur Bottom," were filmed south of the Cuthand Community in Red River County. Remnants of the steel truss bridge seen in the movie still exist and are near the Sulfur River crossing between Titus and Red River Counties near CR 1412.

The husband-and-wife team of Harriet Frank Jr. and Irving Ravetch wrote the screenplay. They made key changes to Humphrey's original story to play up the core conflicts. Captain Wade's illegitimate son would be added, and his wife became a desirable but bitter woman instead of the aging crone from the book. The writers knew how to capture the cadence of southern speech, having previously written another southern family drama, *The Long, Hot Summer*. The film's director, Vincente Minnelli, would later call it "one of the few film scripts in which I didn't change a word."

The roles of Wade and Hannah were originally intended for actors Clark Gable and Bette Davis but later were given to Robert Mitchum and Eleanor Parker. George Hamilton as Theron Hunnicutt (the mama's boy), George Peppard as Rafe Copley (the illegitimate son) and Luana Patten as Libby Halstead (both boys' love interest) rounded out the cast.

Robert Mitchum would win his only major acting award when the National Board of Review named him Best Actor for his work in *Home from the Hill* and *The Sundowners*. Mitchum, who liked to joke that he had "two acting styles—with and without a horse," revealed in this role that he had significantly more to him than that. George Peppard was also named Best Supporting Actor for his performance. Although Captain Wade (Mitchum) portrays the father of Rafe (Peppard) in the movie, Mitchum was only eleven years older than Peppard.

For pickers and antique buffs, the leaded glass lampshade shown in Rafe's living quarters is a Duffner & Kimberly "Owl" lamp and was part of the holdings of the MGM prop department. It was also featured in many other films made by the studio, including *Mannequin* (1937), *Ziegfeld Girl* (1941) and *Young Ideas* (1943). Between the 1930s and the 1960s, stained-glass lampshades had fallen so completely out of fashion that the art department used them to indicate that the home was either poor or unfashionable. Presently, these shades are quite collectible, and one of these D&K "Owl" shades can easily sell for more than $5,000.

Eleanor Parker was reportedly unhappy that Mitchum was getting $200,000 and a percentage of the gross, while she was getting only a flat $75,000. George Hamilton was cast after MGM executives were impressed by his performance in *Crime and Punishment U.S.A.* He explained, "What Vincente later told me he saw in me was not my tortured soul but that I had the quality of a privileged but sensitive mama's boy."

What is it about this movie and book that makes it the quintessential story of Texas and its people? The wealthy cattle rancher or the working cowboy looking for his next paycheck? Most Texans today see at least one of the characters in this epic yarn as like one of their own family, good or bad—be it their favorite great-uncle who owned the local dry goods store or their crazy second cousin who shot the gambler from Vegas in a friendly poker game.

The plot takes you back to the last days of expansive landholdings in Texas controlled by one man—in this case Captain Wade Hunnicutt. In the first movie scene, Wade is duck hunting when he is wounded by a jealous husband. The Captain is a notorious womanizer who lives with his beautiful wife, Hannah, who scorns him. She has raised their son, Theron, to be dependent on her, but as he reaches adulthood, Theron seeks his father's help to learn how to hunt. He has been embarrassed by a group of local hunters and friends of his father who took him on a snipe hunt. For you non-Texans, the hunt ends with Theron crawling on his hands and knees blowing a whistle and trying to coach a nonexistent snipe into his tow sack. He vows to never be the laughingstock again and asks his father for help. His mother is totally against her philandering husband taking the boy under his wing, but Captain Wade puts his foot down. Hannah tells Wade that he can't treat her like one of his hunting dogs sitting around his chair. The Captain snaps his fingers, and the dogs come to attention!

One of the Captain's employees, Rafe Copley (also Wade's illegitimate son), is given the assignment to "make a man out of" Theron. The son admires the slightly older and more worldly Rafe and rapidly develops into a marksman and skilled hunter; he also learns about women from Rafe. Theron even convinces Rafe to ask a girl he favors, Libby Halstead, to go with him to a barbecue at his parents' home, as Theron is too shy to ask her himself. Rafe tells Libby the next time he comes around, he'll be asking for a date for himself.

Theron falls in love with Libby, but her father won't have it because he's aware of Theron's father's reputation as a womanizer. Hannah tells Theron the reason why Libby's father hates him and that Rafe is his illegitimate brother. The Captain won't acknowledge Rafe as anything but a hired hand and a bastard child.

Theron leaves home and rejects both his parents, along with the concept of family and thus Libby, his true love. Libby discovers that she's pregnant, but she won't confront Theron because she doesn't want that to be the reason for their marriage. Rafe comforts Libby and agrees to marry her out of passion and compassion. Theron, who realizes his error, is devastated.

Life in the unnamed town (Clarksville) continues as usual until the christening of the happy couple's newborn son. Libby's father overhears gossip that his daughter was impregnated by Captain Hunnicutt and goes into a rage.

The scene changes. Wade and Hannah are at home trying to reconcile after seventeen years. On his knees before Hannah, Wade pleads, "Forgive me—not all at once, just a little bit every day." While she takes a step toward peace, Hannah's rebuke, "You're too late, Wade, with too little," ultimately ends their story. Hannah leaves the room, and Wade is shot down by an unknown assailant.

Theron tracks down his father's killer and finds it to be Libby's father. The distraught father tries to shoot Theron but is killed instead. Rafe shows up in time to witness the self-defense. Although Rafe objects, Theron decides to leave town, never to return.

The final scene (months later) shows Rafe meeting Hannah at the Captain's grave site. He offers to include her in the life of her grandson, and she shows him that she has acknowledged him as Wade's son on the headstone.

Home from the Hill opened to strong reviews. The film is often recognized as one of the great melodramas directed by Minnelli late in his career. Dave Kehr, a critic for the *New York Times*, cited *Home from the Hill* as a "superb example" of these celebrated melodramas, where "Minnelli's characters don't simply act out their discomfort with the roles they've been thrust into or the relationships they've chosen to endure, but project their feelings onto the visual and aural fabric of the film."

The movie premiered at the prestigious Radio City Music Hall and was the American entry at the Cannes Film Festival. It cost only $1,818,688 to produce and grossed $2,184,558, plus an additional $1 million in foreign rentals. Despite these good box office results, it was not enough to overcome the high production costs for this film, resulting in a loss for MGM of $122,000 (more than $1 million in 2019 dollars), according to studio records.

When I think of the Texas spirit and my chest puffs out with pride, my mind retraces the scenes from this momentous movie, as I ride along with these modern-day trailblazers taming the wild, wild plains of East Texas.

A SMALL-TOWN MIDNIGHT KILLING

HOW A SLICK LAWYER LEFT HIS MARK ON PALESTINE, TEXAS

December 5, 1959, started out like any other day in a small Texas town. People went to work, children played in the yard unattended and everyone thought it was just another day, like the lazy Friday before it. "Mack the Knife" by Bobby Darin was playing on a radio somewhere, and the one window at the box-sized Dairy Queen hadn't opened yet. Teenagers were still grieving over the death of Buddy Holly earlier in the year. But this Saturday night would alter the Mayberry-like persona of Palestine, Texas, forever.

At about 11:30 p.m., Carroll J. Holder (age thirty-one) shot and killed Donald Rex Morris (age twenty-six) about a block from the Anderson County Sheriff's Office and jail. Both men were from well-known families in the area, and the victim's wife was the daughter of the current sheriff, Roy Herrington. The shooter walked up the street to the jail and turned himself in.

Palestine (pronounced *pal*-i-steen) had a population of less than fourteen thousand at the time. Located in East Texas, it is equidistant from the major cities of Dallas and Houston and Shreveport, Louisiana. Today, it is notable for its dogwood floral blooming season, for having twenty-three historical sites in the National Register of Historic Places and as the western end of the Texas State Railroad (a tourist train operating between Palestine and Rusk). In 1960, the chamber of commerce was not happy that a midnight killing had tarnished its idyllic small-town appeal.

Two days later, funeral services for Donald Rex Morris, of 2830 North Jackson, were held at 2:00 p.m. in the Hassell & Foster chapel. Reverend Otis Felton and Dr. W.R. Swain conducted the final rites, and burial followed in Land of Memory Cemetery. The killing had left daughter Rexie Lee (ten months old) without a father.

Site of the 1960 trial of Carroll Holder in Palestine, Texas. *Wikimedia Commons.*

The subsequent trial would not begin for nine months. Tensions remained palpable during this period because almost everyone knew, or was kin, to one of the parties. Andrew and Carrie Holder (Carroll's parents) were faced with one of the toughest decisions any parent can make: what could, or would, they do for their son?

In rode Percy Eugene Foreman, a fifty-eight-year-old lawyer who was in every way as large as Texas. Six-feet-five and close to three hundred pounds, he had hands like catchers' mitts; as one Houston lawyer put it, he had a head that was "simply monstrous, the biggest in town."

However, it was probably his acquittal record and fearlessness that drew Mr. and Mrs. Holder to him. In the 1952 trial of an alleged gangland murderer, Foreman argued that the defendant's confession had been beaten out of him by Harris County sheriff Buster Kern and Texas Ranger Johnny Klevenhagen. As soon as the jury declared the defendant not guilty, the sheriff and the ranger leaped over the railing and proceeded to beat Foreman, who was already using a crutch because of a sprained left knee. Upon his release from the hospital, the injured lawyer grinned and said to the press, "I harbor no malice toward these poor, misguided minions of the law."

Perhaps the reason for hiring Foreman could have been because of a popular Texas saying at the time: "If you shoot someone in cold blood at high noon on a street crowded with witnesses, the first thing you do is call Percy. The second thing you do is figure out how to pay for his services."

Percy Foreman made no bones about the fees he sought, often saying, "The laborer is worthy of his hire—that's scripture." Foreman often accepted cars, diamonds, land and houses in lieu of cash payments. It was soon rumored around town that the Holders had signed a lien on their farm over to Foreman.

For the upcoming trial, Percy was pitted against his 1927 classmate from the University of Texas Law School, Bob Reeves. Reeves had been hired as a special prosecutor for the case by the Morris family. Rounding out the prosecution was Reeves's partner John McDonald, District Attorney Jack Hardee of Athens and Anderson County Attorney Ernest Swift. Local attorney E. Tate McCain Jr. and Luther Jones of Corpus Christi assisted Foreman. District Judge R.W. Williford of Fairfield would preside over the case.

I was ten years old at the time the trial began. My mother would pick me up every day from Lamar Elementary and take me to observe the trial. I can still remember the "show" that Foreman put on and how he impeached the prosecution's witnesses, as well as the resulting laughter from spectators. Apparently, my mother wanted me to be a lawyer, but I turned out to be honest instead!

Jury Selection

A special venire of two hundred persons was notified to appear in Third Judicial District Court on Monday, September 19, 1960, to hear the "murder with malice" case. The courtroom was packed with spectators on the first day. Only two jurors were selected. By noon on the second day, the original two hundred had dwindled to twenty-six, with only two more jurors added. Court recessed at 11:00 a.m. on Wednesday (with only eleven jurors) awaiting the reporting of seventy supplementary veniremen selected from the County's Jury Wheel at the commencement of the previous day's proceeding. Testimony finally got underway at 10:30 a.m. on Thursday after attorneys had picked the twelfth and final juror.

Opening Statements

Foreman's opening statement focused on three points to prove that Carroll Holder killed Donald Rex Morris in self-defense:

- A neck cut that Holder received from Morris the night of the shooting.
- The position of Morris's car at the scene of the slaying.
- Whether or not there were weapons of any kind on Morris or in his car.

Clyde Rhodes, chief deputy sheriff of Anderson County, was the first person to take the stand. He identified four state exhibits presented by the district attorney. They were a .32-caliber pistol, an envelope containing one spent hull and one live round and an envelope containing two empty .32-caliber hulls.

The neck cut came into play as Rhodes described it as "a scratch" in his testimony when he observed the night of the killing. Foreman made theatrical play of the injury, parading his client before the jury box with a magnifying glass over the portion of the neck in question. Percy quipped, "I call it a cut and you call it a scratch."

Rhodes also testified that he had not looked in the car he identified at the scene as belonging to the deceased. Foreman asked him if it had not occurred to him that the car might contain some evidence of the crime: "Didn't you think it was part of your duty, or were you afraid you would find some weapons in that 'son in law's' car?" Rhodes had testified earlier that Morris was the son-in-law of Anderson County sheriff Roy Herrington. He further admitted that it would have been possible for others at the scene to have picked up a weapon if there had been one. The court recessed at 5:00 p.m.

Saturday

The sixth day of trial began with Foreman shadow boxing for almost an hour trying to keep Holder's jailhouse confession from the jury. Anderson County Attorney Ernest Swift testified that he took the confession less than two hours after the shooting and that "Holder had freely and voluntarily made the statement after the proper warning had been given." Judge Williford denied all of Foreman's motions.

In the statement, the defendant confessed that he shot Morris with a .38-caliber pistol. He said that he had known Morris a long time and that they saw each other about 10:00 p.m. that day and had a few beers:

> *We were riding together in my car on the Elkhart Highway. We had been arguing some and when we got to about Pat Cook's store, then I turned around and started toward Palestine. Donald said, "We are going to Elkhart" and I said no we are not. When I said that he cut me on the neck with a knife. I stopped the car and he got out and told me to get out. I drove off and left him standing there.*
>
> *I drove on back to Palestine and continued riding around by myself. I was going west on Avenue A when he came out a street by the Day and Night Grocery in his car and pulled in front of me. I stopped. He got out of his car and came toward me. I got out of my car. Don said he was going to whip me, and he was at that time up to about my car on foot. That is all that happened. I shot him one time. It looked like I hit him in the stomach or chest and he fell to the pavement. When I shot him, he said "Carroll, you've done it" and that was all he said. Then I got in my car and came to the jail. I saw Clyde Rhodes there and told him about it. Then the Sheriff came in and I gave him the pistol.*

The sheriff, Roy Herrington, and his family lived at the jail, so he was probably there when Holder surrendered himself that night at midnight.

The state next called Deputy Sheriff C.H. (Slick) Wilson, who testified that on the orders of Sheriff Herrington, he had searched Morris's car that night and found a whiskey bottle; he had determined the contents to be water after tasting it. On cross-examination, Wilson said that he had not seen any other evidence in the car. Foreman questioned Wilson at great length concerning an Elkhart-area dance pavilion (honkey-tonk) where he had been in the course of his duties the night of the killing. Wilson admitted that he had seen Donald Morris at the pavilion for a brief time.

The prosecution rested, leaving twelve of the witnesses subpoenaed still not heard.

The defense scored on the second of three witnesses called before the court recessed at 5:00 p.m. Roy Ingram was working at the Bratz and Boyd service station on the night in question. He testified that while cleaning the windshield of the car after Morris had stopped for gas, he saw a holstered pistol, a shotgun and two liquor bottles. This was about five hours before the shooting, Ingram added.

Anderson County was "dry" at the time—the government forbidding the sale of any kind of alcoholic beverages. Some prohibit off-premises sale, some prohibit on-premises sale and some prohibit both. Anderson County prohibited both, so alcohol could be important and relative evidence. Palestine went "wet" in 1962.

The last witness to testify that day was Jerry Ward, a student who had been in the vicinity. He said from the witness stand that his car was almost hit by the 1959 white Pontiac driven by Morris only minutes before the incident. His passenger, Bennett Flanagan, got out of the car and ran back to the scene. Ward said he continued to the police station, reported the trouble and then offered testimony as to the position of Morris's car when he returned to the scene.

Both witnesses were challenged on cross-examination by John McDonald as to discrepancies in their testimony from what they had told the grand jury. Both said they did not remember and had no explanation.

Second Week

The passenger in Jerry Ward's car, Bennett Flanagan, was the first witness called by Foreman on Monday morning. Flanagan told the jury that when Ward turned right onto Avenue A, he looked over his shoulder and could see Morris and Holder standing opposite each other in the street. He said he witnessed Morris pull his right arm straight back with his fist clenched, and then he heard two explosions. Flanagan concluded that they were gunshots when he saw one of the men fall.

Flanagan further stated that he had Ward stop the car, and he jumped out and started back to the cars in the road. "I yelled, and Holder looked up like he was startled, then turned around and started driving back up the avenue east." Flanagan testified that he did not hear Morris or Holder say anything.

When he got to the scene, he said he saw "this fellow lying on the ground and the next thing I knew when I looked up, I saw John Frank Armstrong." He said that Armstrong knelt beside Morris, supporting his head so that the wounded man could breathe easier. "A crowd almost immediately began building up," Flanagan observed. Both he and Armstrong testified the 1959 white Pontiac driven by Morris was protruding off Elm Street into Avenue A about half the length of the vehicle. This testimony was intended to support Foreman's contention that Morris forced a showdown with Holder by pulling into the street in such a manner as to block Holder's car.

The afternoon session began with the defense putting Mrs. Bobbie Parker Socia on the stand. Bobbie, a twenty-three-year-old divorcee, testified that she, her mother and two children were headed downtown to see Christmas decorations when Morris pulled up behind her and honked his horn. He parked his car and joined them, bringing along a bottle of liquor. She added that she had known Donald all her life but had not seen him in about six years. At some point, Socia told Morris she thought that he should get out of her car because he was married and she was separated from her husband.

"If you're afraid of Roy [Morris's father-in-law, the sheriff], I'll get out on the hood and ride through the middle of town," Morris told her. It was only a few minutes later that she invited Holder to join them and drive her car. When Morris wanted to go to a dance in Elkhart, Socia said she wanted to go back to Palestine, and Holder turned the car around.

Mrs. Socia testified that Morris waved a knife in front of her after taking it out of his pocket and then reached around her, as she sat in the middle of the front seat, and slashed Holder beneath the left ear. She said Morris then told Holder to stop the car. Morris got out of the car in a hurry and rushed around to the driver's side with the open knife in his hand. She said Morris then tried to open the door, and she asked Holder to drive away and leave him because "I don't want any trouble out on the highway with my babies."

On cross-examination, the prosecution implied that she could have inflicted the cut on Holder herself with a diamond ring that she was wearing. Mrs. Socia, who frequently wept under cross-examination by District Attorney Jack Hardee, said she had dated Holder several times since the shooting but had not dated him prior to that time.

Percy Foreman on re-direct disputed any inference that the ring had caused the injury and passed the ring around the jury for examination.

Tuesday

Otis Alverson, a Knox Glass employee, testified that Morris had pulled a pistol from his pocket and "threatened to shoot the brains out of Paul Simpson" outside an Elkhart dance pavilion shortly before Morris was killed in Palestine later that night. Alverson stated that it was more or less a "drunken brawl" between Simpson, Quinton Prater and Morris and that the men shook hands afterward. Morris then asked the three if they had seen Carroll Holder; Morris said, "Well, I got out of the car too…and that SOB ran off and left me, but I'll find him before the night is over and when I find him, I'll fix him."

If you ever watched *Judd for the Defense* (reportedly based on the career of Percy Foreman) on TV in the late '60s, then you know that the defense never puts its client on the witness stand in a murder trial. At 10:30 a.m. on Tuesday, the eighth day of the trial, Foreman did just that. Carroll Holder, a thirty-two-year-old oil field roughneck who had only a ninth-grade formal education, told the jury that Morris appeared "mad at me" almost an hour before the shooting.

That perceived animosity came to a head about 3.5 miles from the Palestine city limits on the Elkhart highway. Holder testified that Morris cut him on the neck but that he did not see the instrument he was cut with and could not say what it was. Holder's testimony matched that of Mrs. Socia regarding the events that transpired in the car.

"I was excited and afraid," Holder told the jury as he described Morris pulling his car in front of him. There was apparent danger of a collision "if I had kept going straight because he was in my lane of traffic." Holder said he stopped his car, and Morris "slung open the door of his car and rushed toward him." He also said that from the headlights of the car, he could discern Morris's facial expression as mad and mean.

Holder reached into the glove compartment and took out his pistol as Morris was charging, he continued. Holder said that he thought Morris was armed with a knife and that there was not enough available light to see if he actually had a knife. "I did not intend to kill him. I tried to stop him from killing me." When Morris started toward him, the defendant said he warned him to stop.

Holder admitted to firing the revolver twice, the second time into the air because "the hammer had not gone back down." He said he had never previously fired the gun.

On cross-examination by Reeves, Holder admitted that the gun was not his but rather belonged to his sister-in-law, Mrs. William (Lela) Holder. He said she did not know he had the weapon, and he had taken the pistol several days prior to the slaying because he was going to Mineola to see a girl and would be making most of the trip at nighttime.

Reeves got no cooperation from the defendant when he tried to get him to take the revolver before the jury and show exactly how he held it when he shot Morris. Holder refused and said he could not do so. Holder said on questioning by Reeves that he would not have shot Morris in order to avoid a fistfight, but he said he was no physical match for the victim.

Holder said under cross-examination that he stopped his car at the scene of the shooting and did not attempt to swerve and pass around Morris's car because "if I had turned to the left and gone on Donald would have run me down anyway." Holder also said he "had been afraid of Donald Morris ever since I had known him."

The defense rested at 4:00 p.m., and the prosecution began putting rebuttal witnesses on the stand. Quinton Prater and Paul Simpson, the two men who according to earlier testimony had trouble with Morris outside an Elkhart dance hall, both testified that they had not seen a pistol in Morris's hands that night and that he had not made a threat to blow the brains out of Simpson. Foreman countered the testimony on cross-examination by going to great lengths and theatrics to imply that both Prater and Simpson were so intoxicated that night they didn't know what was going on.

George Hutcherson testified that a pistol and shotgun seen in Morris's car earlier on the night of the slaying belonged to him. He went on to say that they had been out shooting quail and at buzzards during the afternoon of that day and that he removed the weapons from the car when Morris took him back to his place of employment.

Roy Mathis, a Palestine policeman who was at the scene of the slaying the night it occurred, testified that Morris's car was not pulled out into the street far enough to impede the progress of another vehicle.

The trial moved into its ninth day (Wednesday), with the prosecution continuing to call rebuttal witnesses. C.W. Maupin, a chemist with the Department of Public Safety in Austin, testified that the examination of the sweater Morris was wearing showed "nitrate particles." Maupin explained that from this evidence, he had calculated that the muzzle of the pistol that hit Morris was greater than three feet and less than five feet from the victim. Special Prosecutor Bob Reeves offered this testimony to impeach the defendant's story as to the distance at which the gun was fired.

The Prosecution's Case

District Attorney Jack Hardee opened the closing argument for the prosecution. He told the jury that Holder could not believe that his life was in danger just before he shot Morris and that he did not use all means except retreat—one of the main points of this case. Hardee said that Morris invited Holder to ride in the car that night. He also questioned

Mrs. Socia's testimony that she could see (because of lack of light) Morris cut Holder on the neck or that she could see Morris run around the car. The district attorney described the cut as "not even serious enough to be treated by a doctor."

"He could have stayed in the car," Hardee stated. "It is unlikely that a man could whip another in a car when a gun was being held on him."

Percy Foreman's Closing Argument

To an overflow crowd in the courtroom, Percy Foremen took the next four hours to carefully characterize the victim of his client's pistol as the product of a society for which he was not entirely to blame. "Somebody failed to plant in the mind and heart of this boy at an early age the advantage of training his mind and equipping himself for the struggles of life."

The Houston attorney showered the state's witnesses with flowery words of praise while at the same time undermining the credibility of their testimony. He questioned how Holder could have been indicted in the first place: "From the evidence you have heard in this case, you have the right to assume that he was indicted for the same reason he was unable to obtain the counsel of his choice in this county…influence."

Foreman noted that testimony established that Donald Morris habitually bore a gun: "To me that more aptly personifies the type of individual that departed this life in Anderson County on December 5, 1959, more than any other factor." He called Morris a "King Kong of a man" and added that all he knew was "the law of the jungle—the survival of the fittest."

"We usually find what we look for," Foreman commented. "Clyde Rhodes was not looking for anything that night because he was afraid of what he would find, but let's not be uncharitable by the hindsight, unless we can put ourselves in his position"

In an unusual observation, Foreman admonished the people of Palestine for not providing more places of wholesome entertainment to occupy the spare time of their young men and women. "When Carroll was riding on Avenue A that night, he was doing evidently what appears to be an established practice for passing time in Palestine."

Poetry and scripture were liberally sprinkled in his argument, and Percy seldom raised his voice. He often took out an old pocket timepiece and wound it as a distraction. After the trial, he admitted that the watch hadn't kept time in years.

When the trial started on Thursday morning, Foreman was still making his lengthy argument. He would use three more hours (seven hours total) to bring his defense of Holder to a close.

The Verdict

Special Prosecutor Bob Reeves required only thirty minutes to rebut Foreman's exposition and wrap up the case. He told the jury that it had come to him during the defense's argument that "he was using the jury just like a harp." Reeves pleaded that the case should not be decided "on flattery or scripture but exactly on what was in Holder's mind at the moment he pulled the trigger."

The experienced lawyer hammered on Holder's confession and how it had changed in his testimony after hiring Forman to defend him. He specifically mentioned the matter of the .38-caliber pistol in the confession, when the death weapon was actually a .32-caliber. Addressing the jury, Reeves pleaded, "Here is a confessed murderer and Percy is trying to appeal to your egotism!"

The jury returned its verdict of "not guilty on the charge of murder with malice" one hour after receiving the case at 3:00 p.m. W.J. Inmon, foreman of the jury, said only two ballots were taken. The jury had sent out at 3:55 p.m. for the .32-caliber revolver used in the killing and the confession that Holder made the night in question. No other requests were made from the jury room until they told the judge they had a verdict.

Applause greeted the announcement of the verdict, but it was quickly squelched by Judge R.W. Williford, who had warned against any such demonstration.

It had taken ten working days to hear this epic trial in Palestine. An overflow audience had filled the vaulted, second-floor courtroom every day. It brought an end to the naïvete of the '50s for most of the residents. Most folks agreed that it was "bad choices" that brought Carroll, Bobbie and Donald together on that fatal night. "It was a big deal," one local resident explained sixty years later. "I don't think Palestine was ever what Andy and Barney would call their 'hometown' after that."

OSWALD'S LAST PHONE CALL

The following series of events was unknown to the Warren Commission (the official investigation authorized by President Johnson) in 1963–64. This information would not become publicly known for twenty-five years.

On Saturday, November 23, 1963, the day after President Kennedy was shot in Dallas, Alveeta Cave Treon, a forty-three-year-old telephone switchboard operator, arrived at work on the fifth floor of the Dallas Municipal Building. She came in early (about 10:25 p.m.) to relieve Louise Swinney, another operator who had asked to leave early. Mrs. Swinney was seated near one end of the ten-position switchboard. Mrs. Treon took a position near the other end, leaving about four to six seats separating them. She had no idea that the next thirty minutes would place her in the history and lore of Kennedy assassination conspiracies.

Lee Harvey Oswald, the suspected assassin, was being held in the Dallas Police Department's portion of the building on a lower floor. As soon as Mrs. Treon, the 11-7 shift operator, sat down to begin work, Mrs. Swinney told her that two men would be coming up to the switchboard to listen to a call. She went on to say that the call would be placed by Lee Harvey Oswald. Mrs. Swinney made it quite clear that their superiors had sent instructions for them to cooperate with the men.

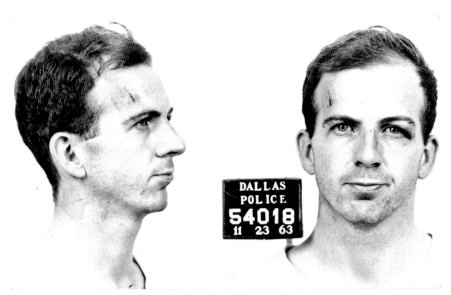

Dallas Police Department arrest card of Lee Harvey Oswald, 1963. *Wikimedia Commons.*

About ten minutes later, a knock came to the door, which was kept locked at night for security purposes. Mrs. Swinney, the closest to the door, unlocked it. Two men identified themselves to her. In later testimony, neither woman could remember if the gentlemen were city, state or federal law enforcement officers, but they let them into the equipment room.

A red light came up on the board, showing a call from the jail. Both operators plugged in simultaneously to take the call. Mrs. Treon was the first to say, "Number, please," but it was Mrs. Swinney who took charge of the call. Mrs. Treon said later, "I did not unplug. I quit trying to handle the call and let her, but I stayed plugged in with my key open." Mrs. Treon could hear everything that was being said by Oswald:

> *I heard her repeat a number to the caller and saw her write down details on a notation pad, which is normal routine. She then closed the key so no one on the line could hear her, then called the two men in the room on a line and said that Oswald was personally placing his call....I listened and watched very carefully for Mrs. Swinney to place the call with the long-distance operator. She appeared very nervous and visibly shaken. For a few minutes, she just sat there trembling.*

Instead of making the call, Mrs. Swinney opened the key to Oswald and told him, "I am sorry, the number doesn't answer!" In 1988, Surell Brady, a senior staff counsel for the House Select Committee on Assassinations (HSCA), summarized Mrs. Treon's version of events this way:

> *Mrs. Treon stayed on the line. She said she was, therefore, able to hear everything Oswald said and she is sure he asked for the name John Hurt and gave the two numbers. She said that as she listened she wrote the information down on a regular telephone call slip. However, since Mrs. Swinney actually handled the call, Mrs. Treon signed her [Mrs. Swinney's] name to the slip she intended to keep as a souvenir. She said the notations on the slip of "DA" and "CA" stand for did not answer and canceled because the call was never actually put through. Mrs. Treon said she never retrieved any paper from the wastebasket on which Mrs. Swinney supposedly entered the information. Had Mrs. Treon not kept the LD call slip that she filled out as a souvenir, this story would be no more than the most minor of footnotes in the tragedy of the Kennedy Assassination.*

However, years later, when the identity became known of the man to whom Oswald was trying to place a call, its significance would rise to the "very troublesome" and "deeply disturbing" levels ascribed to it by HSCA chief counsel G. Robert Blakey.

The (919) 834-7430 number in 1963 belonged to John D. Hurt of Raleigh, North Carolina. No evidence exists that Oswald and Hurt ever met or that there was a direct connection. However, a man possibly facing the death penalty does not call a perfect stranger with his only phone call.

What if Oswald was following a set intelligence practice (tradecraft), consisting of contacting his case officer through what is known as a "cut-out"—an intermediary who can act as a "safety line" without ever getting involved in the operation itself. All the "cut-out" knows is that if anyone calls, he's then to contact a predetermined person or agency. The "cut-out" can legitimately say he never heard of the asset calling.

According to committee records, Mr. John David Hurt seems to have had an unusual career, but aside from his counterintelligence work in the Second World War, there is nothing to confirm or deny his candidacy as Oswald's "cut-out."

EARLE CABELL: DALLAS MAYOR OR ASSASSINATION CONSPIRATOR?

Earle Cabell was the mayor of Dallas, Texas, on November 22, 1963, when President Kennedy was assassinated. What most Texans don't know is that he was secretly a paid CIA asset (since 1956) and that he sat in on planning sessions for JFK's visit, where he urged minimal security precautions for the motorcade limousine. This astonishing fact only became a matter of public knowledge in 2017, when President Trump declassified additional secret government documents that had been sealed since 1963.

Earle was born in Dallas on October 27, 1906. He was the fourth of four sons of the then former Dallas mayor (1900–1904) Ben E. Cabell. His older brother Charles Pearre Cabell, born in 1903, would become deputy director of the Central Intelligence Agency in 1953 and was serving in that capacity when Earle was recruited. In 1962, Charles was forced out

JFK motorcade in Dallas, Texas, on Main Street, November 22, 1963. *Wikimedia Commons.*

of the CIA by President Kennedy as retaliation for the agency's epic, failed military invasion of Cuba known as the "Bay of Pigs" disaster.

Mayor Cabell and his wife met President John F. Kennedy and First Lady Jackie Kennedy at Love Field on the morning of November 22. Mrs. Cabell reported that while riding in Kennedy's motorcade through Dealey Plaza, she observed "a rather long looking thing" sticking out of a window of the Texas School Book Depository immediately after the first shot. After receiving death threats, Cabell was guarded by police when he traveled to Washington, D.C., to attend Kennedy's funeral and upon his return to Dallas.

Of the many conspiracy theories that have cropped up over the last fifty-five years, this revelation gives new credence to the "Renegade CIA Clique" hypothesis. This cabal implicates the Cabell brothers and other alleged conspirators, including CIA officials James Jesus Angleton and William King Harvey, in the assassination. In fact, it claims that Earle Cabell rerouted Kennedy's motorcade as a favor to his brother. This is sobering. It "illuminate[s] that the CIA's extraordinary penetration of domestic American institutions extended to the city where JFK was killed," said renowned assassination researcher Jefferson Morley. "If anyone had said over the past 50 years that the mayor of Dallas in 1963 was a CIA asset, they would have been derided as a 'conspiracy theorist.' Now we know for a fact that he was."

In Vincent Michael Palamara's book *Survivor's Guilt*, published years before either Palamara or the general public knew that mayor Earle Cabell was a CIA asset, we learned that Earle not only participated in the planning for Kennedy's Dallas visit but also urged that security precautions for JFK be as minimal as possible and that agents not be posted on the rear of the limousine.

Stewart Stout, one of JFK's Secret Service agents on the Dallas trip, died in 1974 without ever being interviewed by the Warren Commission or the FBI. In 2010, Stout's son wrote to author Palamara: "Though I would mention that one of the influential people that attended the advance planning meetings for the Dallas trip was the Mayor of Dallas in 63 and I think it was Earle Cabell....I distinctly...remember during a conversation at the dinner table weeks following (that surreal day), my father telling my mother that 'the Mayor thought agents riding on the back of the car (which was a common protocol) would send a message and [he] did not want his city to appear dangerous to the world through the media. He asked for subtle security exposure if and where possible.'"

Most security experts believe that President Kennedy probably would have survived the sniper attack if (as was usual during presidential motorcades) Secret Service agents had been standing on the rear steps of the limousine.

History has yet to tell us who made the decision not to have agents on the rear of the limousine during that fatal motorcade. It had been reported that some of JFK's protection detail blamed Kennedy for his own death, claiming that a few days before the Dallas visit, Kennedy ordered agents not to position themselves on the limousine's rear steps—and that he had done so for flippant reasons. This story has since been debunked.

Despite the twenty-five-year deadline established by the 1992 JFK Records Collection Act, not all the Assassination Files were released. Citing national security concerns, President Trump elected to halt the release of some of the remaining classified files. The president said he was ordering agencies to "re-review each of the redactions over the next three years" and set a new deadline for further release of documents for October 26, 2021. I can't wait!

I ATE THE LARGEST WHITE PERCH
EVER CAUGHT IN TEXAS

February 14, 1968: Garvin Goy Wooderson is fishing on Lake Navarro Mills in typical Texas weather. The low is 32° in the morning with slight misting rain, but the afternoon sun will take it up to a bearable 48°. His Chrysler boat and motor are tied up to a group of stick ups and he is facing away from the wind. A bottle of Jim Beam is keeping the minnow bucket company near a worn life jacket. Not exactly the best fishing weather but a record-setting day for this fisherman and this lake.

On that day, G.G. (Boots) Wooderson, my second cousin, broke the Texas State Record for white crappie, catching a monster fish weighing 4.56 pounds!

Boots (a nickname earned as a child) commonly referred to this species of fish as "white perch," as did many people in southern states. The fish is from the genus *Pomoxis*, North American freshwater fish in the sunfish family *Centrarchidae*. The name derives from the Canadian French *crapet*, which refers to many different fishes of the sunfish family. Other names for crappie include papermouths, speckled bass or specks (in Florida), speckled perch, strawberry bass, calico bass (throughout the Mid-Atlantic states) and *sac-a-lait* in southern Louisiana. For purposes of establishing state records, the Texas Parks and Wildlife Department recognizes two species in this genus: white crappie, *P. annularis* (Rafinesque, 1818), and black crappie, *P. nigromaculatus* (Lesueur, 1829). Regardless of the name, this fish is considered by most fishermen in Texas to be excellent table fare.

Boots was ahead of his time when it came to fishing techniques for white perch and other fish. Before the first float tube was ever commercially produced, Boots had a local saddle shop construct a canvas cover for a large tractor inner tube with a seat in the middle so that he could float out to spots to deep to wade. He used a small wooden paddle tied to the tube to move among the bushes and rushes as he picked apart the openings for waiting fish. When he got too old to safely use the tube, he gave it to me.

Lake Navarro Mills was one of Boots's favorite fishing destinations. Located near his home in Corsicana, this U.S. Army Corps of Engineer's project covers 5,070 acres on Richland Creek, a tributary of the Trinity River in Northeast Texas. The project began in 1959 and was completed in 1963. The lake was primarily built for flood control and to supply the water to the residents of Navarro County.

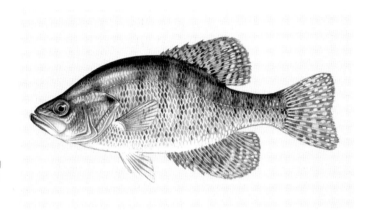

This fish with many names (*Pomoxys sparoides*) is excellent table fare. *Wikimedia Commons.*

Immediately upon catching the new record, Boots nicknamed the giant fish "Big John," after the popular song of the same name sung by Jimmy Dean. Unlike the fisherman of today, my second cousin didn't mount the fish or have a fiberglass replica made. Instead, "Big John" went under the knife and ended up in the freezer.

Fileting white perch in the 1960s was considered wasteful by many fishermen, especially those who grew up in the Great Depression. Boots and my father were raised "poor" in Grimes County, Texas, near Bedias and survived the tough times by hunting and fishing. If they caught it or killed it, they ate it.

Usually, Boots scaled and gutted his catch, cut out the dorsal fin and placed the remaining whole fish in a wax milk carton, making sure it was completely covered in water before freezing. Obviously, at nearly five pounds, "Big John" was too big for this and ended up cut up into dozens of filets and frozen. At our next family outing to Boots and Charlene's (we lived in Palestine), Boots thawed out the filets and cooked them in white cornmeal on a gas burner in the backyard. My parents and I enjoyed a fantastic supper. As Boots summed it up later over a cold Miller High Life, "It don't get no better than this!"

Boots Wooderson's record catch has held up for more than fifty years but is under assault most days, as fishermen continue to search for this tasty freshwater jewel. The Texas record for black crappie was caught by George Ward on Lake Fork as recently as April 27, 2003, and weighed 3.92 pounds. Rumors of big catches and giant crappie permeate most of the fishing camp stories around the six thousand lakes in this state. But as of this writing, I can still say, "I ate the largest white perch ever caught in Texas!"

MISS EDNA'S FASHIONABLE RANCH BOARDING HOUSE

On November 27, 1961, Edna Milton bought a farmhouse for $28,500 from her employer, Fay Stewart, known in the county as "Aunt Jessie." Originally from Oklahoma, Edna officially named the place Miss Edna's Fashionable Ranch Boarding House in the legal paperwork. Tucked back amid the post oaks and cedar trees just beyond the city limits of La Grange, Texas, less than one mile off State Highway 71 on an unpaved road, Miss Edna's opened for business and would take in boarders for the next twelve years.

The community immediately took to Miss Edna and appreciated the fact that she kept the business running after Aunt Jessie had to retire. She contributed $10,000 to the local hospital in $1,000 annual installments. She also contributed $1,000 to the community swimming pool and sponsored a Little League team.

Miss Edna was a no-nonsense proprietor. She created a mimeographed booklet and distributed it to all new boarders. She even had a truncated version of the rules painted on plywood and displayed prominently in the kitchen area. A sample of these "Rules and Regulations" follows (spelling and punctuations is as written by Miss Edna):

1. I, Edna Milton, a femme sole trader own this building and all the furnishings, also 11,32 acres of land duly recorded in the Fayette County Courthouse, La Grange, Texas 78945. This place nor I have any connection what so ever with any other place, mob, or syndicate of any type. Any one having no intentions of following these rules might just as well leave now.

2. Absolutely no narcotics are permitted on these premises. If any narcotics are found or suspected the law will be called immediately. Drinking is not permitted during visiting hours and any one doing so will be asked or ordered to leave. In short dope heads, pill heads and drunks are not permitted to live here regardless of who they are.

3. Thieves, liars and robbers are not needed or wanted here when I ask a boarder a question I demand an honest to the point answer.

4. I don't like cliques in my house and I don't want to walk into anybodies room and see a group of people on a bed, chairs or on the floor. Beds are not to be wallowed in. That is what hogs do.

Hand-colored lithograph of a bird's-eye view of La Grange, Fayette County, Texas, in 1880. *Wikimedia Commons.*

5. *There are nine rooms here and I consider it as hiring short of boarders where there are only boarders here.*

6. *No boarder will have a regular room unless I have told her otherwise also at my discretion there may be two boarders in one room, this comes under my business and I don't care to discuss the reason for doing with any one.*

7. *Any time a boarder regardless of who she may be decides to interrogate me in any manner she may show proper credential and a badge authorizing her to do so and then get out.*

8. *The phone is to be used by everyone here I don't want any boarder to receive more than one phone call per day. Anyone caught discussing my business on the phone won't live here. Money is not to be discussed on the phone at any time.*

9. The cook comes to work at 11:00 a.m. and breakfast is served shortly there after. Food is removed from the table by 12:30 p.m. Dinner is served at 4:00 p.m. or shortly there after. No one is to skip a meal because they have company and then expect their food later. I don't pay the cook to cater to anyone, interference with the cook irregardless of which boarder they will leave here as soon as I know about it.

10. All boarders dressed and properly made up by 1:00 p.m. when guests are permitted into the house. Casual dress is appropriate for daytime. All boarders are to be dressed in dinner dresses, cocktail dresses or evening pantsuits no later than 7:00 p.m. I could stay here writing forever but I consider the foregoing rules sufficient at this time, there are of course many other things to be considered and I expect a girl to ask me or whomever is in charge.

Miss Edna's little place would continue to be famous over the next dozen years. But bad publicity in the summer of 1973 would cause Sheriff J.T. Flournoy, a longtime friend, to tell her "she was no longer allowed to operate." Flournoy then went to Austin to meet with the governor, armed with a petition opposing the closure including three thousand signatures. Dolph Briscoe refused to meet with him.

The Texas Chamber of Commerce chose to ignore the closing of this establishment possibly older than all its members, and the State Historical Society, equally misguided, overlooked the boarding-up of a house that slept more politicians than the Driskill Hotel and the Governor's Mansion combined.

Miss Edna's Fashionable Ranch Boarding House was the basis for a 1978 musical on Broadway and adapted to the big screen in 1980 starring Dolly Parton and Burt Reynolds. Rock band ZZ Top was inspired to write a ballad about it called "La Grange" in 1973. Some people even went so far as to proclaim that Miss Edna's place was the "Best Little Boarding House in Texas"!

Recollections of a Prison Siege

The 1974 Carrasco Incident in Huntsville, Texas

The last shot was fired as I walked up the steps to the Huntsville Unit, more commonly known as the "Walls" because of the tall red brick exterior. I had been called to come in early, as I was assigned to a later shift. That shot would mark the end of the longest siege of a prison at that time in American history. That eleven days at the Texas Department of Corrections (TDC) in Huntsville, Texas, would become a tragedy for this small town. Two inmates were killed, a priest was wounded, two teachers lay dead and a correctional officer became an unpretentious hero.

Wednesday, July 24, 1974—Day one would start out just like any other day at the Walls. Wednesday was the day that grand juries from around the state would tour the unit. There was one scheduled from West Texas that day, but it had been canceled. It is believed by some that Carrasco picked this hour to strike because he wanted to capture jurors, who were not employees of the prison.

I worked across the street at the administration building but normally ate at the officer's mess, located under the Education and Library facility on the west side of the upper yard in the Huntsville Unit. That day, I chose to eat with some good friends in town.

Gunshots, partially muffled by the daily 1:00 p.m. whistle, alerted correctional personnel to the initial takeover of the library by inmates Fred Gomez Carrasco, Rodolfo Dominguez and Ignacio Cuevas. One of the shots hit Sergeant Bruce Noviskie in the foot, but he was able to get away and was not seriously wounded.

The three armed inmates took everyone in the facility hostage and within the first hour established telephone communications with Warden Hal Husbands. Hostages included a correctional officer, sixty inmates and ten teachers from the Windham School District, a TDC rehabilitation program. Subsequently, fifty-six inmates were released from the library. Father Joseph O'Brien entered to temporarily act as a mediator. The library had only one entrance, so it became a fortress for the trio demanding their freedom.

Initial demands of the three hostage-takers included three M15 rifles, six bulletproof vests, three bulletproof helmets, five clips for each rifle, three hundred rounds of ammo, fifteen pairs of handcuffs and a television. Only the television and handcuffs were delivered to the library under siege.

The "Piñata," as it was called by prison officials, or "Trojan Taco," as it was dubbed by the news media. *Author's collection.*

Late in the evening, teacher-hostage Glen Johnson suffered an apparent heart attack and was allowed to leave the library. Total hostage count was now fourteen, including ten employees (not including Father O'Brien) and four inmates.

Personnel were soon assigned twelve-hour shifts. I was stationed above the warden's office on the night shift with a view of the library entrance, which was the only way in or out. One of the teacher-hostages was always secured on top of metal file cabinets blocking access. This was a sniper position. The designated sniper from the Ferguson Unit (also the dog sergeant) was assigned to our shift. I was part of a team that would protect and debrief the hostages at the end of the ordeal.

THURSDAY, JULY 25, 1974—Day two continued the negotiations between TDC director W.J. Estelle Jr. and Fred Carrasco, the obvious leader and former narcotics kingpin from San Antonio, Texas. Threats of executing the hostages continued throughout the day, but the deadlines imposed by Carrasco passed without incident. By the end of the day, Father O'Brien was considered a hostage.

FRIDAY, JULY 26, 1974—Day three would include additional demands and threats. Helmets and walkie-talkies were given to Carrasco. Officials offered national media coverage if the trio would surrender peacefully. In the early evening, seven shots rang out, five in the library and two that struck the nearby prison chapel. No shots were returned, and no breaching attempt was considered. Officials were confident that no one had been injured yet. Carrasco was granted his first telephone interview with a San Antonio newsman.

SATURDAY, JULY 27, 1974—Day four resulted in officials agreeing to new helmets (constructed to Carrasco's specifications), belts and holsters, as he complained that the previous helmets supplied were not satisfactory. Construction of the new helmets began at the TDC mechanical shop. The rest of the day consisted of telephone interviews by press representatives with the hostage-takers and telephone conversations between hostages and their families.

SUNDAY, JULY 28, 1974—Day five was another day of media interviews with both the hostage-takers and the hostages. An average of eighty members of the press were on site to cover the incident. This was my first brush with the kind of reporters who will make up a story if they don't have one to print. I witnessed a media type get into a confrontation with an officer guarding the doors to the administration building. The angry defender of the "fifth estate" stormed off in a huff and shouted, "Don't you know we're for the convicts anyway!"

One of the specially designed helmets was completed and given to Carrasco for inspection. The prototype was acceptable, and he asked for two more.

MONDAY, JULY 29, 1974—Day six would break the monotony of waiting and bring everyone to high alert. At about 5:30 a.m., an excited voice came over the radio: "They're coming out, they're coming out!" An inmate hostage had jumped through the plate glass in the library doors and escaped. Apparently, his nerves got the best of him, believing that Carrasco thought he was a "snitch" and was going to kill him. After what seemed like an eternity (probably two minutes), the "all clear" came over the radio. I turned to the sniper from Ferguson and said, "What did you see through the scope?"

After he started to breathe again, he replied, "Nothing but confusion!"

Later in the day, hostage Aline House was allowed by the gunmen to be taken out of the library, apparently having suffered a heart attack. This left the count in the fortress at ten employees, three inmate-hostages and Carrasco, Cuevas and Dominguez.

TUESDAY, JULY 30, 1974—Day seven was a long day and, in my case, a long night. The dog sergeant kept everyone awake by telling stories about his dogs and the "chases" that resulted from inmates attempting to escape. In eleven days, I learned more about bloodhounds than I thought I would ever need to know, but it certainly helped fight the boredom from looking at one doorway all night.

Negotiations throughout the day centered on the demand for bulletproof vests, with the threat to set off homemade bombs placed on or near various hostages. The Texas Board of Corrections voted down a proposal by the gunmen to exchange the hostages for Director Estelle, a TDC assistant director, Warden Husbands, Major Murdock and any captain in the prison system. At about 2:00 p.m., gunshots were heard in the library, but it was determined that no one was injured.

WEDNESDAY, JULY 31, 1974—Day eight would bring new demands from Carrasco. He demanded transportation and stated that four hostages would leave with him. The remaining nine hostages were to form a shield as the escapees made their way to the waiting vehicle. Threats for failure to comply with his demands continued throughout the day.

THURSDAY, AUGUST 1, 1974—Day nine included enhanced demands for transportation out of the unit. Carrasco requested an armored car equipped with short-wave radio and a regular telephone. A blackout was placed on media coverage due to concerns for the hostages' lives amid the sensitive negotiations that were taking place. This resulted in one of the hostage's daughters holding an outside press conference to relay messages from Carrasco to the press. The temperature that day was ninety-three degrees.

FRIDAY, AUGUST 2, 1974—Day ten would result in the release of another hostage. At about 6:15 p.m., Linda Woodman, a teacher-hostage, came running down the ramp from the library. Carrasco wanted her to explain the details of his escape plan to TDC officials. Her release came after increased tensions affected the negotiations due to an electrical storm that had knocked out all power to the library, eliminating lighting and air conditioning to the fortress.

SATURDAY, AUGUST 3, 1974—Day eleven would forever change the lives of many of the unwitting participants in this siege and attempted prison break.

The decision was made in the morning to intercept the armed hostage-takers attempting to escape as they descended the stairs from the library. In the early evening, an armored car (a cash transport vehicle) equipped with two-way radio communication was parked in the upper yard at the foot of the ramp to the library. An inmate hostage carried personal possessions and "bombs" to the waiting escape vehicle. As he returned on the last trip, he placed trash cans across the north ramp to warn of a rush from that side.

Huntsville fire truck units outside the west wall supplied fire hoses, brought into the dining hall just below the library. The interception team, led by Texas Ranger captains Pete Rogers and G.W. Burks, along with FBI agent observer Bob Wiatt, took up their positions in the dining area.

Earlier, Carrasco had provided officials with blueprints of their initial escape contraption, referred to as a "Piñata." It was constructed from large blackboards, books, tape and other materials from the library areas. Carrasco also provided information as to the makeup of the shield. Hostages Yvonne Besada, Julia Standley, Novella Pollard and Father O'Brien would be inside the Piñata, handcuffed to the armed escapees. The remaining five employees and three inmate hostages would be handcuffed to the outside to form a shield.

Carrasco sent out an inmate hostage to make a last check of the area before beginning his departure. At about 9:15 p.m., the "Piñata" slowly left the library. The first and second turns were made without incident, but after the third turn, the contraption high centered on the ramp and could not move.

A stream of water under high pressure from the fire hoses was turned on the "Piñata," as the interception team began its assault. Calls to surrender were made but were answered by gunfire from inside the blackboards. Return gunfire ensued.

Out of nowhere, TDC lieutenant Willard Stewart from the Coffield Unit crawled to the "Piñata" and then, taking out his pocketknife, cut the rope binding the hostages on one side and then crawled to the other side and freed those hostages. They all scattered to safety. Stewart was not on the interception team, but like other heroes of our time, he saw a need and acted without regard for his own life. Later, he would say that he turned his back to the blackboards so that he wouldn't see it if he got shot.

Gunfire continued from inside the "Piñata," and the interception team returned fire, careful to aim at the muzzle flashes. The fire hose lost water pressure and failed to topple the escape vehicle, but the interception team was able to topple it by pushing with a ladder. The final shots rang out.

Yvonne Besada and Julia Standley, teacher-hostages inside the "Piñata," died at the hands of their captors. Father O'Brien was critically wounded. Miraculously, Novella Pollard was unhurt. The other employee-hostages—Bertha Davis, Ann Fleming, Ron Robinson, Anthony Branch and Bobby Heard (the only correctional officer)—were freed without injury.

Our team was immediately dispatched to the administration building to take care of the hostages' families. What can you say? Syndicated columnist Cal Thomas, who was an on-site reporter for Houston's KPRC-TV at the time, later wrote, "None of us who were there for those eleven incredible days will ever forget the tension, the heat, the frustration, and the courage of so many good people, inside and outside that prison. It is a tragedy that two hostages died. It is a miracle all the rest lived."

The narcotics kingpin of San Antonio, Fred Gomez Carrasco, died from a self-inflicted gunshot. Rudolfo Dominguez raised his hand with a gun in it from the pile of bodies. Father O'Brien yelled, and immediately DPS officer Winston Padgett shot Dominguez twice. He died instantly. The last gunman, Ignacio Cuevas, was unhurt and taken into custody. Cuevas was given the death penalty and was executed on May 23, 1991 (seventeen years later).

W.J. Estelle Jr. would comment to the press later that day:

> *At no time was any thought given to granting illegal freedom to the captors….We could never in good conscience ever turn such violence loose on the community of Texas….We owe our fine staff that small degree of insurance provided by the knowledge that the act of taking hostages will not provide the means of escape….No hostage taken through our gate would have any chance for life.*

GOLDEN SWEET POTATOES

OPRAH WINFREY, HAROLD AND ANNETTE SIMMONS AND KACEY MUSGRAVES

The Oprah Winfrey Show on October 28, 2004, "Oprah's Favorite Sandwich," concluded with a segment she called her "Best of Everything" list. The sweet potato was at the top of Oprah's choices. In fact, she went on to explain:

Now, I just have to tell you about one more of my favorite foods. Harold and Annette Simmons are my dear friends and neighbors in California although they live most of the time in Dallas. Dahhh-lus! Everyone says "Dahhluss." Well, they know how much I love sweet potatoes and a while back Annette sent me a bunch.

It turns out that Harold Clark Simmons, the American businessman and billionaire, was born in Golden, Texas. Simmons, who died in 2013 at age eighty-two, was famous for developing the acquisition concept known as the leveraged buyout (LBO) to acquire various corporations. He was the owner of Contran Corporation and of Valhi Inc. (a NYSE traded company about 90 percent controlled by Contran). In June 1980, Harold married his third and last wife, Annette Caldwell Fleck, a native of Tyler, Texas, and a graduate of Southern Methodist University. In 2001, Harold and Annette purchased an estate next to Oprah in Montecito, California.

Oprah continued:

I was having one for a snack. I love sweet potatoes and I'm telling you it was pure heaven. They have found the purest, sweetest sweet potatoes, the best sweet potatoes I've ever had. And so, I called Annette and Harold right away to ask, "Where on earth did you get these sweet potatoes?" Turns out they're from a small Texas town, where sweet potatoes are so popular they even have their own special day.

The Golden, Texas Sweet Potato Festival is held during the fourth week in October each year. It all began in 1982, when Monty Montgomery, a local radio station owner, came up with the idea of a community-wide get-

East Texas sweet potatoes (*Ipomoea batatas*) on display at the annual Golden Festival. *Wikimedia Commons.*

together once a year to raise money for the repair and upkeep of the Golden Community Center, now known as the Harold Simmons Community Center. Not only did Harold and Annette attend the festival for many years, but their patronage has also helped to sustain the tradition—thirty-five years strong and still growing.

Two events, a cooking contest and an auction of boxes of sweet potatoes grown by local farmers, were the meager beginnings of the festival. Two flatbed trailers were joined together to form a makeshift stage for the sweet potato and food auction. By 2004, when Oprah aired her show, the festival had grown to include a parade and entertainment at the pavilion, and the top bidders at the auction got their picture made with Miss Texas.

Annette told Oprah on the live feed:

> There are only nine sweet potato farmers here, and most of them are third-generation farmers. Each year they harvest about 2 million pounds of sweet potatoes. Oprah, the highlight of the Sweet Potato Festival is the auction. And it raises more than $30,000, and the proceeds go to needy families in Golden.

Oprah is not the only star to find Golden, Texas, but it was much easier for singer/songwriter Kacey Musgraves—she was born there!

"Wherever you grow up really shapes you a lot," Musgraves said during a phone interview for the *Fort Worth Star Telegram* from her home in Nashville. "But in a small town, word gets around about who you are. There's something really transparent about living in a place like that. There's an aspect about that that really inspires me."

The Golden memories are apparent in her hit record "Dime Store Cowgirl." The song is autobiographical and recounts memorable moments in her meteoric rise to country music stardom, including having her "picture made with Willie Nelson" and drinking wine she "can't afford."

Kacey first appeared at the Golden Sweet Potato Festival as a nine-year-old, yodeling the oldies in fringy western wear. She returned in 2012, marking her first time back to the festival since her debut single, "Merry Go 'Round," started moving to the top tier of the country charts. Kacey's mother booked this homecoming gig to celebrate the opening of her new art gallery. Like in most East Texas families, saying no to mom isn't even a consideration. In April 2014, Musgraves won the Academy of Country Music award for album of the year for *Same Trailer Different Park*.

The allure of Golden and the fascination of the Sweet Potato Festival was best captured when Oprah, on her award-winning show, noted that there were about twice as many people in her audience as there are in the whole town of Golden.

ONE TOWN'S LOSS IS ANOTHER CITY'S TRAGEDY

Vernon Wayne Howell was born on August 17, 1959, in Houston, Texas. His mother, Bonnie Sue Clark, was only fourteen years old, and his father, Bobby Wayne Howell, left her for another teenage girl before he was born. They were never married. Vernon never knew his father and was raised by a "mean stepfather."

Vernon described his early childhood as very lonely. Because he had dyslexia, he was a poor student and dropped out of high school. It was alleged that he was once raped by older boys. The young Howell had not been successful in school, but by age twelve, he had learned the New Testament by heart.

During his teenage years, Vernon was moved around East Texas, looking to improve the influences in his life. He lived with his grandmother Earline Clark in Chandler, but when he turned eighteen, he moved to Tyler, Texas. When he was nineteen, Vernon got a sixteen-year-old girl pregnant, but she left him because she considered him unfit to raise a child. He then became a born-again Christian at a Southern Baptist Church. Their teachings were not exactly to his likings, so he joined his mother's church, the Seventh-day Adventist Church.

It was here that he fell in love with the pastor's daughter. One day, while praying for guidance, he opened his eyes and found the Bible open to Isaiah 34:16 and the

Vernon Wayne Howell, age fourteen, before his spiritual transformation. *Retrieved from https://www.who2.com/ david-koresh-and-the-waco-siege, Paul Hehn, 2012.*

words, "none should want for her mate." Vernon was convinced that this was a sign from God, so he approached the pastor and told him that God wanted him to have his twelve-year old daughter as his wife. The pastor was livid, and when Howell continued to persist in the pursuit of the child, he was expelled from the church. A member of the congregation is reported to have explained that Vernon never "thought above his belt buckle."

Next, Howell joined a religious group originating from a schism in the 1950s of a group called the Shepherd's Rod (themselves excommunicated members of the Seventh-day Adventist Church in the 1930s). In 1983, Vernon began claiming the gift of prophecy. He then had an affair with Lois Roden, the prophetess and leader of the sect who was then in her late sixties. Claiming that God had chosen him to father a child with her, Howell further prophesized that this would be the "Chosen One." By 1983, Roden began allowing Vernon to teach his own message, which caused controversy in the group. Lois Roden's son George, originally intended to be the group's next leader, considered Howell a false prophet. In the ensuing power struggle, George Roden, claiming to have the support of most of the group, forced Howell and his group off the property at gunpoint.

Howell and about twenty-five followers then set up camp at Brushy Creek near Palestine, Texas, where they lived under rough conditions in buses and tents for the next two years, during which time Howell undertook recruitment of new followers in California, the United Kingdom, Israel and Australia. That same year, Howell traveled to Israel, where he claimed he had a vision that he was the modern-day Cyrus.

The location of Howell's cult was often referred to as a compound, but most of the good folks around Palestine believed they were a bunch of "hippies" and little was known about their beliefs. Howell would often send children to neighboring homes to gather water, and over time, the community's consensus shifted from concern to annoyance. It wasn't long before these complaints caught the attention of Gary Thomas, the newly elected sheriff in Anderson County. Thomas sent deputies to Brushy Creek to talk to the cult. This agitated Howell, and he went to speak personally with Sheriff Thomas.

In an interview with KETK TV, Thomas recalled, "[Howell] brought this guy with him who claimed to be his attorney. I asked him if he was a real attorney and he kind of looked at me, so I asked for a Texas Bar card and he couldn't give me that. So, I invited him to leave and go sit in the lobby."

After this meeting, Thomas learned all he needed to know about Vernon Howell: "He surely didn't like any authority figure going out there trying to tell him what to do.…He felt that he should be able to live out there and do exactly what he wanted and didn't want to follow the law, or the rules or whatever you want to call them."

The sheriff wasn't too excited about the goings-on at Brushy Creek until the local manager of Walmart told him that Howell's cult was buying all the guns they could from the store. A local gun store owner also confirmed that they were purchasing significant amounts of firearms.

"Automatic weapons is what they were looking for," recalled Thomas. "So, you know, you've got concerns when you've got someone living out in the woods in a situation like that and they're buying automatic weapons. As the sheriff of this county, it was concerning."

Back at the camp, Howell made sure that everyone was forced to rely on him and him alone. Previous bonds, family or otherwise, meant nothing. Howell believed that if his flock had no one to depend on, they had to depend on him—and that made them vulnerable. It was at this time that he began to give the message of his own "Christhood," proclaiming that he was "the Son of God, the Lamb who could open the Seven seals."

Then, one day in 1985, Howell packed up his followers and left Anderson County. Vernon Wayne Howell filed a petition in California State Superior Court in Pomona on May 15, 1990, to legally change his name "for publicity and business purposes." On August 28, 1990, Judge Robert Martinez granted the petition. The name change arose from his belief that he was now head of the biblical house of David, from which Judeo-Christian tradition maintains the Messiah will come and that he, too, was an anointed one like Cyrus.

The end of the journey of Vernon Wayne Howell (now called David Koresh, with "Koresh" being a transliteration of the Hebrew name Cyrus) is synonymous with the darkest day in the annals of American law enforcement. On February 28, 1993, the Bureau of Alcohol, Tobacco and Firearms (ATF) raided the Mount Carmel home of David Koresh and the Branch Davidians near Waco, Texas. The ensuing gun battle resulted in the deaths of four agents and six Branch Davidians. The siege of Mount Carmel ended fifty-one days later, on April 19, 1993, with seventy-nine Branch Davidians dead, including David Koresh; twenty-one of these victims were children under the age of sixteen.

During the siege, Koresh would explain to the FBI negotiators that (in his twisted mind at least) "Koresh" had a deeper meaning:

> *Koresh: "What is Christ revealed as, according to the fourth seal?"*
> *FBI: "Pale…a rider on a pale horse."*

Koresh: "And his name is what?"
FBI: "Death."
Koresh: "Now, do you know what the name Koresh means?"
FBI: "Go ahead…"
Koresh: "It means death."

HAVE YOU BEEN EVERYWHERE (IN EAST TEXAS)?

In 1996, Johnny Cash had a popular hit called "I've Been Everywhere." This contagious, knee-slapping melody was not the first time this song had been recorded. The song was written by an Australian country singer named Geoff Mack in 1959 and was made popular by Lucky Starr in 1962.

The song, as originally written, listed Australian towns. Geoff Mack's music publisher offered the tune to Canadian-born country musician Hank Snow. Snow thought the song had potential for the Canadian and American markets, but only if the toponyms were adapted to North America. At his publisher's urging, Geoff Mack consequently rewrote the song using a North American atlas supplied to him by the publisher. "I've Been Everywhere" was a number-one U.S. country hit for Hank Snow in 1962. In addition to Johnny Cash, the song has been recorded by various artists, including Lynn Anderson (1970), Asleep at the Wheel (1973) and Kacey Musgraves on her album *Movin' On* (2003).

Have you been everywhere? Of course not, but have you been everywhere in East Texas? For instance, have you been to Crow, Texas? This community is located at the intersection of Farm Road 778, U.S. Highway 80 and the Missouri Pacific Railroad, fourteen miles southeast of Quitman in southeastern Wood County. It was originally called Graham when a railroad station was built there in 1876. The town received its first post office in 1906 and was renamed Crow in honor of Wilson Crow, who worked at a local sawmill. Crow at one time had several stores and a saloon, reported to be the last saloon in Wood County.

In the 1930s, Crow had a population of one hundred, a church, three businesses and a school that, in 1932, had an enrollment of eighty-eight students in nine grades. At that time, Crow was still a station on the Texas and Pacific Railway. By 1956, the post office had closed, and the church and

You can go anywhere in East Texas if you follow the signs. *Author's collection.*

school were closed by 1960. Over the next decade, the population gradually declined, and the 1970 census reported the population at twenty-five. It was the same for the census of 2000.

Just three miles northeast of Crow and less than a mile west of Lake Hawkins on Farm Road 2869 is the town of Fouke. A community called Center was said to exist in this area in 1866, and sometime around 1873, the inhabitants built a log building. In 1879, a two-acre site for a Methodist Episcopal church was bought for six dollars. The pastor of this church also taught the school, which was attended by black children only. A school district for black students was established in Center when Wood County was divided into public school districts in 1884. The name of the town was changed to Fouke sometime after 1885, when George W. Fouke's lumber company built a large sawmill in the area.

By 1932, the school had an enrollment of 17 white students and 111 black students, and there were two churches and a few widely scattered dwellings. When Lake Hawkins was formed by a dam on the Little Sandy Creek sometime after 1960, several new dwellings appeared in the town, which now supported two businesses and a town hall. The population was 30 in the year 2000.

Hainesville is another spot in the road you may not have visited in Wood County. Located at the intersection of Farm Roads 49 and 778, seven miles southeast of Quitman, this area became famous in 1870 when excavations were being made for the Haines mill. By 1893, the post office at nearby Dupree had been moved to the community and was now called Hainesville, after Haines, whose family owned the mill and a general store. The town of twenty-five was now served by a blacksmith, a cotton gin and three music teachers. A Methodist church probably hosted the community's first school, which in 1896 reported fifty-one students. In 1907, the post office closed, and by 1968, the population was seventy-four, the same level as reported later in 2000.

Or you might want to drive by Redlands, Texas. Located at the intersection of Farm Roads 778 and 3056, Redlands, also known as Weimer (Weimar) and Macedonia, is within the old Martin Varner land grant, which is said to be the site of the earliest white settlement in Wood County. The Wood County Historical Commission placed a marker near the site of the Varner homestead and cemetery, thought to be the first cemetery in Wood County.

Other small towns in Wood County include Cartwright, Concord, Holly Lake Ranch, Liberty, Mount Pisgah, New Hope, Oak Grove, Peach, Perryville and Pine Mills. I think Hank Snow, Johnny Cash and Kasey Musgraves might have passed through Golden at one time or another!

ABOUT THE AUTHOR

T ex Midkiff is a writer, storyteller, local historian and a retired VP of an international security concern. Peter Ellis Bean, the husband of his ancestor Candace Midkiff, came to Texas with the Philip Nolan expedition in 1800 when it was still "New Spain." Tex's love of Texas and East Texas history has its roots in these early settlements.

Candace Midkiff Bean's 1936 Texas Centennial Marker reads in part: "One of those pioneer women who braved the menace of Indians and frontier life and rocked the cradle of Texas liberty."

Baptized in the Trinity River and raised in the piney woods of East Texas, Tex is the consummate mythical male Texan. His roots are firmly planted in the sandy loam, coveted by the likes of J. Frank Dobie, John Henry Faulk and Larry McMurtry. You might even call him the "Ditto-Head Antonym" of Molly Ivins!

Tex is published—some of his best work appears in newspapers and magazines, and he has previously written three books: *Divorce Made SIMPLE (In 100 Difficult and Very Expensive Lessons)*, *Some People Call It (Poetry)* and *The Midkiffs: Early Tejas Settlers and Sons of Old Virginia*.

A "featured columnist" for the *Community Chronicle* and *Fencepost* magazine, Tex and his wife, LaJuana, reside at Lake Fork near Yantis, Texas.